S0-BBD-291

Common Ground

Managing and Understanding Workplace Diversity

Edited by National Press Publications

NATIONAL PRESS PUBLICATIONS

A Division of Rockhurst University Continuing Education Center, Inc.

6901 West 63rd Street • P.O. Box 2949 • Shawnee Mission, Kansas 66201-1349

1-800-258-7248 • 1-913-432-7757

13984729

National Press Publications endorses nonsexist language. In an effort to make this handbook clear, consistent and easy to read, we have used "he" throughout the odd-numbered chapters and "she" throughout the even-numbered chapters. The copy is not intended to be sexist.

Common Ground: Managing and Understanding Workplace Diversity

Published by National Press Publications, Inc. with contributions from
Jan Lewis and Micki Holliday

Copyright 2001 National Press Publications, Inc.
A Division of Rockhurst University Continuing Education Center, Inc.

All rights reserved. No part of this publication may be reproduced or utilized in any form by any means, electronic or mechanical, including photocopying, recording or by any information storage and retrieval systems, without permission in writing from National Press Publications.

Printed in the United States of America

1 2 3 4 5 6 7 8 9 10

ISBN 1-55852-196-8

About Rockhurst University Continuing Education Center, Inc.

Rockhurst University Continuing Education Center, Inc. is committed to providing lifelong learning opportunities through the integration of innovative education and training.

National Seminars Group, a division of Rockhurst University Continuing Education Center, Inc., has its finger on the pulse of America's business community. We've trained more than two million people in every imaginable occupation to be more productive and advance their careers. Along the way, we've learned a few things: what it takes to be successful ... how to build the skills to make it happen ... and how to translate learning into results. Millions of people from thousands of companies around the world turn to National Seminars for training solutions.

National Press Publications is our product and publishing division. We offer a complete line of the finest self-study and continuing-learning resources available anywhere. These products present our industry-acclaimed curriculum and training expertise in a concise, action-oriented format you can put to work right away. Packed with real-world strategies and hands-on techniques, these resources are guaranteed to help you meet the career and personal challenges you face every day.

Table of Contents

INTRODUCTION

The metamorphosis overtaking the workforce today is creating enormous demand for change. Organizations are faced with challenges:

1. Constantly changing technology

2. Globalization

3. Increasing diversity in the workforce

The exponential bursts of knowledge and an increased dependency on connectivity have made us closer than ever before to every corner of the world. We currently live in a "global village," as Marshall McLuhan called it. The world, in its great variety, now spills into our schools and communities and is reflected throughout our workplace.

Because of advances in medicine and the aging of the baby boomers, born between 1946 and 1965, the number of older adults will rise to record levels. According to the 2000 U.S. Census, by the year 2015 one in six Americans will be 65 or older. Most of the baby boomers will be retired or near retirement. And a whole generation of millennium babies will be approaching adulthood. By 2020, one in six Americans will be Hispanic. That number will increase to one in four by midcentury.

The barrier to success that is in greatest need for redress is people's discomfort with those different from them. The need going forward is to find common ground among groups of different ages and different cultures. Race, gender, sexual orientation, ethnicity, education, social and financial status — all demand different interpretations. Sensitivity to different sexual identities and nontraditional lifestyles is vital. Actually, this tremendous diversity in America can serve our nation well as it strives to compete in the global economy.

Several components of diversity follow:

- The demographics of today's workforce have changed drastically within the last generation.

- Recruitment needs require effective management of diversity.

- Retention demands diversity to be handled positively.

- Productivity is an inherent result of diversity.

- Teamwork is enhanced by diversity.

- Globalization requires appreciation of multiple cultures.

- Legal and compliance pressures are increasing.

As a member of the workforce, the key to surviving and thriving in the future is to embrace the differences. Keep your mind open to others who are different from you. Move away from stereotypes and thinking ruts; increase reason and awareness, for yourself and your organization. Train yourself to avoid conflict and to foster real collaboration. Get involved in groups and activities that are racially, ethnically and culturally diverse. Learn to communicate effectively with others. Doing these things will lead to understanding and appreciation of what makes each of us unique. They will also lead to respect for each individual. This handbook will show you how to adapt to diversity and be comfortable with those different from you.

The goals of this book are as follows:

- To recognize the influence on behavior of one's perceptions and opinions

- To realize how reactions to diversity can affect performance and organizational effectiveness

- To develop an understanding of the differences inherent in people

- To analyze the benefits that diversity brings to an organization

- To strengthen skills in dealing with the differences of people

- To create a plan for capitalizing on diversity within the workplace

Most importantly, this book is a wake-up call. The world is changing; education does breed tolerance; and success is based on innovation, different approaches and diversity! Whose responsibility is it to foster these new perceptions, and to challenge stereotypes and biases and inaccurate generalizations? It is yours and mine. The time is now; the critical mass is here.

1 A BUSINESS CASE FOR DIVERSITY

Diversity touches every aspect of our lives, even our children's lives, from raising children to outperforming the competition. Crayola announced in 1999 that it would find a new name for its "Indian Red" crayon. The company decided to make the change even though it said the color name came from a paint pigment found near India and not American Indians. JoAnn Chase of the National Congress of American Indians applauded the action, saying it "underscores the American public's growing sensitivity." Several years ago, Crayola also altered the name of its "Flesh" crayon, dubbing it "Peach" instead.

Pitney Bowes was recognized in 1994 with the Catalyst Award, and in 1998 by *Working Woman* magazine for its representation of women at all levels of employment. The company exceeds industry averages — over 40 percent of the direct reports to their chairperson are women. Likewise their global agenda emphasizes a strategic commitment to diversity — supporting minority-owned and women-owned businesses and leveraging their unique workforce through innovative leadership.

Slowly, but surely, corporate America is recognizing the importance and value of diversity. It's smart management to draw upon the richness of diversity and help all employees do their best work. Diversity awareness and management and resourceful leadership are the keys to discovering the hidden potential in each worker.

But how can you actually put principle into practice and begin integrating diversity into your company? The process has three key steps:

1. Diversity awareness. This means seeing and appreciating what makes each worker unique as well as understanding that a variety of perspectives can make your company stronger. Working together successfully in a diverse environment should be the ultimate goal of awareness.

2. Diversity management. This means making sure every worker has the chance to contribute to company goals. The company must attempt to build a mutually satisfying relationship with each worker. Management practices to allow this include recruitment, discipline, coaching and performance reviews that reward the promotion of diversity.

3. Resourceful leadership. For diversity to become a business asset, individuals must demonstrate tolerance, appreciation and the art of turning conflict into collaboration. Leaders must model their values and bring others with them in living the principles of respect and appreciation of differences.

These are lofty goals that can't be accomplished overnight. Blending diversity into the workplace takes both time and commitment. It happens subtly, through an evolution of thoughts and actions rather than through a mandate that dictates, "From this point forward, all employees must adhere to the blending policy." Realistically, it can take at least a year from the time the company incorporates diversity awareness training until actual changes in the work environment are realized. It must be done, however. This isn't a social issue; it's a business imperative.

The Argument for Diversity

Projected workforce shortages mandate that companies recruit more minority, immigrant, senior and disabled people to fill job openings. This is compounded by the fact that the baby boomer generation is inching toward retirement, and current families are having fewer children to take their places in the years ahead. During the decade of the 1970s, the labor force grew by almost 3 percent annually. That figure shrunk to 1 percent during the '90s.

As recently as 1995, over 70 percent of Americans were Caucasians, according to *Workforce 2000: Work and Workers in the 21st Century*. By the year 2050, that percentage rate is expected to fall to below 50 percent, a decrease of more than 20 percent. In contrast, the percentage of Latin Americans will increase by about 12 percent during that same time span, from approximately 10 percent in 1995 to more than 25 percent in 2050. The percentage of Asian-Americans will more than triple, while the percentage of African-Americans will grow by a modest 2.4 percent. The American Indian population will remain about the same.

These statistics prove what may seem obvious: More and more people with widely diverse backgrounds are working together. According to the *Workforce 2000* study, 85 percent of those entering the U.S. workforce between 1985 and 2000 have been women and minorities. The Hudson Institute and the Department of Labor revealed startling changes in workforce composition: U.S. born white males comprised less than 20 percent of the new entrants into the workforce in the year 2000. They made up 7 percent less of the workforce than a decade prior and are fast losing their traditional position as the dominant component of the workforce. Managing and incorporating these changes into the corporate culture have become both our greatest challenge and our greatest opportunity.

In short, the workplace of today is vastly different from the one that Henry Ford knew. It is vastly different from that of our parents! Groups outside the traditional mainstream make up increasing portions of organizations. Because of what the American workplace is going to look like in the years to come and because of what's happening in society as a whole, we need processes to ensure equal treatment, equal time and equal access for all workers. Organizations are more willing to deal with what were once considered taboo topics and many are requesting training on harassment, violence in the workplace, sexual orientation and disabilities.

These are business imperatives: Productivity and ROI (Return on Investments) depend on valuing the differences. Bottom line, there just are no other workers!

Changes and shortages in the workforce also have made career development more critical than ever before. Continually we hear the cry for talent, skilled labor, and people with even a basic education. Reading, writing and arithmetic skills are becoming as hard to find as computer technology skills were in the '90s. Managers must help workers identify their skills, interests and strengths and then guide them toward the most appropriate careers. Racial or gender stereotypes or old biases could cause managers to push someone down the wrong path. For instance, don't assume that an Asian-American is best suited for a high-tech position or that a woman is best qualified for clerical work. The assumption that "you can't trust anyone who is ... ," whether it is about age, race, ethnicity or whatever, will quickly remove you from any chance for success.

Most experts say that nontraditional is in fact the norm today. We must go beyond whatever differences exist in order to build a talented and capable workforce. What ultimately enhances the bottom line is acknowledgment of individual traits and characteristics that make a person a part of a whole, and because of that belonging, allow him to make a significant contribution to the work. DaimlerChrysler is an example of a company committed to enhancing its enterprises by creating an inclusive environment that values teamwork and inspires all employees — in the U.S. 20+ percent of whom are women and 27+ percent are people of color — to work with passion and enthusiasm.

This is the business case for diversity.

In 1990 there were only five organizations in the entire United States that provided domestic partner benefit programs. By 2000, there were 3,368 companies offering these benefits. The numbers are growing because of the demands of society that businesses deal fairly with people. An honest day's work for an honest day's pay. Changes like these are occurring because talent is at a premium. A tough job market requires that an organization be as attractive to the broadest range of candidates conceivable. The cost of benefits like these, when compared to the return on investment represented by these employees, is practically nonexistent.

An index that is used in recruiting circles is a gay index. This is an indication of the number of gays and lesbians in a community. Whereas gays are no more or less talented than heterosexuals, their presence within an organization or city is a sign of openness and acceptance, values espoused by many sought-after recruits as well as companies seeking creativity. Diversity, then, is a tool to address unemployment challenges.

In a 1998 *Mosaic* article, "Finding New Talents in a Tight Market," the author reported that the disabled virtually languish in an unemployed state while the marketplace screams for their talent. The article notes that as high as 74 percent of people with severe disabilities are unemployed, 70 percent of blind or visually impaired people are under- or unemployed, and 25 percent of mildly or moderately disabled people of employment age are unemployed. This underutilization is not due to their disability; rather, it is because we are not fully integrating them and their many talents into our organizations. Diversity offers a vast, untapped pool of talented, eager and available workers at a time when the workforce and initial competencies are minimal.

Legal Considerations

In addition to a changing labor pool and a shrinking talent base, there's another important reason to practice diversity in the workplace. Job discrimination is against the law. Equal employment opportunity is guaranteed by law, mandated by the U.S. government, and one of several laws designed to promote the recruitment and advancement of "protected class" or minority workers. There are numerous statutes, legal decisions and guidelines that govern discrimination and have a profound impact on all employment and personnel practices. A worker or group of workers can file a complaint under any one or combination of the following statutes:

- Fifth and 14th Amendments to the U.S. Constitution

  The Fifth and 14th Amendments deal with criminal prosecution, due process of the law and eminent domain. A person can't be prosecuted unless there is probable cause, can't be tried twice for the same crime, or be compelled to testify against himself. Further, every person is provided protection, and legal precedent must be followed before property can be taken or the person convicted of a crime. The 14th Amendment makes due process binding to the states. It says no state can pass any laws that deprive any person of rights they have under the U.S. Constitution. It preserves equal protection under the laws. These sections of the Constitution form the legal foundation for diversity.

- Civil Rights Acts of 1866, 1870 and 1871

  These acts prohibit discrimination against a person due to race, religious persuasion and gender. Over 100 years ago, our nation saw diversity as a desirable way to live.

- Equal Pay Act of 1963

  This requires equal pay for equal work in the same establishment for both sexes. It prohibits employers from paying employees of one sex less than employees of the opposite sex for equal work on jobs that require equal skill, effort and responsibility, and are performed under similar working conditions.

- Titles VI and VI of the 1964 Civil Rights Act

  This act prohibits discrimination in all employment practices because of race, color, sex, religion or national origin. It established the Equal Employment Opportunity Commission (EEOC), an agency that advises and assists persons and other agencies with alleged violations of Title VII. Title VI prohibits not only overt discrimination, but also practices that are fair in form but discriminatory in operation.

- Age Discrimination in Employment Act of 1967 (amended)

  This prohibits discrimination against candidates and employees, aged 40–70, in terms of hiring, compensation, discharge, and other major aspects of employment.

- Equal Employment Opportunity Act of 1972

  This act amended the 1964 Civil Rights Act and expanded the investigative power of the Equal Employment Opportunity Commission to cover state and local governments. The 1972 amendments gave the EEOC the power to go directly to court to enforce the law. This act specifies that an employer may not, because of a person's race, color, national origin, religion or sex, refuse to hire, discharge, harass, otherwise discriminate against an individual with respect to compensation, terms, conditions or privileges of employment, limit, segregate or classify his employees in a discriminatory manner nor retaliate against an employee because he filed a complaint, testified or opposed any practices forbidden under the act.

- Civil Service Reform Act of 1978

  The Civil Service Reform Act of 1978 (CSRA) contains a number of prohibitions, known as prohibited personnel practices, which are designed to promote overall fairness in federal personnel actions. The CSRA prohibits any employee who has authority to take certain personnel actions, from discriminating for or against employees or applicants for employment on the basis of race, color, national origin, religion, sex, age or disability. It also provides that certain personnel actions cannot be based on attributes or conduct that do not adversely affect employee performance, such as marital status and political affiliation.

- Vocational Rehabilitation Act of 1973

  This protects the rights and opportunities of the disabled. It specifies that an employer cannot exclude from participation, deny benefits of, or subject to discrimination an otherwise qualified disabled individual under any program receiving federal financial assistance.

- Pregnancy Discrimination Act of 1978

  This prevents gender discrimination on the basis of pregnancy, birth or related situations. It requires the employer to treat men and women the same. Women cannot be discriminated against because they have babies.

- Americans With Disabilities Act of 1991

  Often called the most sweeping piece of legislation in American history, this act extends protection to the disabled by noting that employers cannot discriminate based on disability of any kind. An employer cannot hire or fire on the basis of any type of disability, mental or physical. Substance abuse or addiction is considered a disability under this act.

- Family and Medical Leave Act of 1993

  This act grants family and temporary medical leave under certain circumstances. It is provided to both male and female employees. This act continues to be molded to society and the times, including adoptions, father and mother rights, care of the elderly, illness of a child or custodial responsibility.

- Immigration Reform and Control Act of 1986

  This prevents discrimination if an employee is not a citizen. There is a fine line in the law concerning the hiring and firing of legal vs. illegal immigrants. Legal immigrants, those with a green card, are to be treated like all other employees. Illegal immigrants have no rights and are to be deported.

- Consumer Credit Protection Act of 1973

  This prevents firing if wages are garnisheed. It also prevents firing a person because of any one single debt.

These statutes, and more, attempt to correct a historical pattern of undervaluing and discriminating against a diverse workforce. They focus on issues of race, gender, ethnic background, disabilities, age and more.

Affirmative action involves quotas and is not a part of these laws, as some people believe. Instead, affirmative action requires a company to try to improve the numbers of these protected workers at various levels and positions within the company. For example, if you find minority underrepresentation among your company's middle managers and no apparent reason for it, affirmative action says you should try to correct the situation within a reasonable amount of time. However, any job candidate you choose also should meet the legitimate qualifications for an open position. So consider affirmative action as a flexible goal, not a mandatory quota.

The terms "affirmative action" and "diversity" often go hand in hand, but they are two separate things. Affirmative action, or the practice of hiring minority workers, is only one part of a company's broader diversity plan. Think of diversity as providing variety, while affirmative action attempts to provide an equal and fair blending of that variety.

Dr. R. Roosevelt Thomas Jr., an author and diversity advocate, defines managing diversity as establishing a work environment where the full potential of all employees can be tapped as an organization searches for a competitive advantage and where all employees are judged on the quality of their contributions to the organization.

Temporary Workers

Even temporary workers can sue a business for discrimination or harassment, according to a December 1997 ruling by the Equal Employment Opportunity Commission. Microsoft workers are one example of a group of employees who challenged the rights of their employer to discriminate based on part-time status. Previously, there was a clear distinction between the rights of a full-time person and a part-time person.

This change has come about in part because there are increasing numbers of temporary workers on the job today. The National Association of Temporary Staffing Services reports that its numbers have more than doubled since 1991 and that there are more than 2.6 million temps at work. Furthermore, a 1995

Bureau of Labor Statistics study shows that African-Americans and women make up most of the temporary workforce. This employment category increasingly has become a status of choice.

According to the EEOC's guideline on the issue of discrimination or harassment, liability is determined by who controls the temporary worker's assignments, schedule and working conditions. In some cases, it's the temporary agency; in others, it's the hiring company; sometimes it's both of them. Determining control can determine liability if a temp sues. For more information on this subject, check out the Internet Web site www.eeoc.gov.

To ensure that your company complies with this EEOC guideline, extend your current nondiscrimination policies to cover temporary workers. Treat them the same way you do your own employees. And be sure to take any discrimination or harassment charges filed by a temp very seriously. All charges should be investigated thoroughly and corrective actions taken.

Liability

Most managers understand that they can be held liable for discriminatory actions made against their employees. However, managers may not know that they and their companies also can be held liable for discriminatory actions between other employees if they don't try to resolve the conflicts. This puts managers in a difficult position. Here are eight guidelines to help managers reduce potential liability for themselves and their company.

1. Respond to and investigate thoroughly all reports of discrimination and harassment immediately.

2. Put a stop to any and all workplace rumors.

3. Ask advice from the legal department or human resources and labor relations professionals whenever unusual situations arise.

4. Screen all job applicants carefully and investigate any instances of inappropriate conduct that appear in their background checks.

5. Conduct all of these investigations discreetly.

6. Follow up with the victims of discrimination and harassment. Tell them about the actions taken and ask them to report any future occurrences.

7. Take steps to prevent and correct instances of discrimination and harassment.

8. Encourage all employees to work together.

A 1999 survey of 100 human resources executives by Assurance International, the University of Miami and the American Mediation Institute found that the vast majority of companies are taking strategic action to prevent the risks associated with employee lawsuits. Some survey results follow:

- 86 percent of U.S. companies have written human resources manuals

- 63 percent have begun providing training on employee lawsuits to their managers and supervisors

- 57 percent have employee grievance policies

- 48 percent have purchased Employment Practices Liability Insurance, protection against workers who claim discrimination or wrongful termination on the basis of race, sex or disability

The Impact of Valuing Diversity

The final reason for valuing diversity is that it is measurable: It clearly maximizes performance and increases results. Diversity allows organizations to gain a competitive advantage. It positively impacts operational goals at a level of strategic importance. Behavioral measures calculate the impact on perceptions and demonstrate to the company such successes as increase in customer-satisfaction index, improvement in positive comments on feedback forms and surveys that express high customer-service ratings.

Activity-based measures can account for actions that support various initiatives. Examples are the number of employees who attend diversity training, the number of minority- and women-owned suppliers identified in a certain period, and the number of recruits referred by community partners in a certain period.

Value-added measures show an organization the financial impact of diversity. For example, diversity practices can demonstrate reduction in lost-productivity cost, account for the value of fee advertisements, reduce the cost of hiring, increase revenue due to diversity, and reduce cycle-time costs.

These scorecards can easily note the multiple benefits to an organization for embracing diversity. High performance, breakthrough results and, ultimately, competitive advantage are achieved goals when diversity practices are in place. Aligning human capability creates an environment where people want to work and do their best, allowing organizations to realize results.

The Xerox Model: A Case for Diversity

Xerox is considered a top company for minorities and women. As one employee explains: "If you don't value diversity, you can't manage it." Although Xerox's approach to valuing and managing diversity far exceeds mere affirmative action compliance, it wasn't always that way. Several events led to worker complaints and prompted the company's desire to diversify its workforce.

Senior management at Xerox conducted an internal investigation that showed employees' complaints were legitimate. Something had to be done immediately. So, the company initiated and has since modified a diversity awareness and training program that focuses on five main issues.

1. Listening and communication

2. Coaching, mentoring and counseling

3. Employee compensation

4. Performance improvement

5. Career development

Since 1971, Xerox's diversity awareness and training program has helped managers learn to better interact with employees regardless of their race, gender or cultural differences. In addition, the company started African-American, Hispanic and women's focus groups to provide valuable feedback to management. But the real reasons the Xerox plan worked was the company's commitment, which was based on the following three principles:

1. Adopt a long-term process instead of a quick-fix process.

2. Allocate the human and financial resources needed to make the change.

3. Consider affirmative action a business priority, not just a staff function.

Consider using the Xerox model to build the case for diversity in your company. Building a commitment to diversity training and awareness now will pay big dividends to your company in the next few years.

Answer the following questions about your company or organization.

- What demographic changes are you currently experiencing in your company or organization?

- What impact do these changes have on you and your work environment?

- What is the biggest challenge your organization faces today?

- What changes do you anticipate in the next two to five years and why?

- What must you and your company or organization do to strategically prepare for these changes?

- How would you describe the mix of people within your organization?

- How can you better utilize diversity in your work environment?

Reflections

Chapter 1 Summary

Corporate America is increasingly recognizing the necessity as well as the value of diversity. It's good management to draw upon the richness of diversity and to help all employees do their best work. There are three key steps for valuing diversity: diversity awareness, diversity management and resourceful leadership.

Projected workforce shortages in the years ahead will result in companies recruiting more minorities, immigrants and disabled people to fill job openings. In addition, America's population will continue to grow more diverse. The pool of talented and capable workers is radically changing.

Another important reason to practice diversity in the workplace? Job discrimination is against the law. Affirmative action and equal employment opportunity laws are mandated by the U.S. government and are designed to promote the recruitment and advancement of "protected class" or minority workers, whether they work full- or part-time.

Managers can be held liable for discriminatory actions made against their employees and in cases where they don't try to resolve discriminatory actions between other employees. To avoid situations like these, make sure that you

- Respond to and investigate thoroughly all reports of discrimination and harassment immediately.

- Put a stop to any and all workplace rumors.

- Don't think twice about seeking advice from your company's legal department or human resources and labor relations professionals.

- Screen all job applicants carefully.

- Conduct all of these investigations discreetly.

- Follow up with the victims of discrimination and harassment.

- Take steps to prevent and correct instances of discrimination and harassment.

- Encourage all employees to work together.

2 THE TWO SIDES OF DIVERSITY

Because each of us views diversity through our own eyes, we can develop blind spots. Regardless of the culture to which we belong, we develop insensitivity and inaccurate assumptions. The more dominant the culture, the more convinced we are of our own perceptions. Native English-speaking employees, for instance, may not think it's really necessary to have bilingual or pictorial signs posted at work. Similarly, workers may not fully understand the need for laws protecting workers of the opposite sex from the threats of sexual harassment. Being aware of diversity and seeing it from both sides are first steps toward erasing personal blind spots.

In the U.S. we have traditionally supported a belief that people should "learn to fit in." Known as assimilation, immigrants, women and minorities have received clear messages like these: "Learn our language," "This is how things are done," and "It's our way or the highway: You are in America now!" These messages worked until large numbers of diverse workers challenged them. The '60s and the civil rights movement and Vietnam began valuing opposing thoughts and promoting differing opinions. Today, most companies accept the fact that "different is normal," and assimilation is becoming more and more unacceptable as a dictate.

A definition of diversity is as complex as its implications. And, the definition given is important because it influences internal dimensions within an organization. Some define diversity in the context of the laws, with regard to race and gender or in terms of protected classes. These distinctions — race, gender, protected classes, the disabled, the various statuses that define people

— are important. They can also be limiting and not inclusive of other external dimensions like personality and characteristics.

To best appreciate the benefits and concerns that organizations face today with diversity, it is best to define it in broad terms by its various names: variety, multiplicity, complexity, differences, innovation, change, novelty. An organization can then narrow the focus in terms of what it wants to accomplish by embracing the differences and similarities that people bring into it. We suggest defining diversity as valuing the differences within.

To understand the many complexities of diversity, take a look at yourself first. Where do you fit into the mosaic of humanity? Ask yourself these 10 questions:

1. What are my racial, ethnic and cultural backgrounds?

2. What socioeconomic class do I belong to?

3. What levels of education and training have I attained?

4. What do I associate with my gender?

5. With what generation do I associate?

6. What is my sexual orientation or identity; what are my biases?

7. Have I been classified with any physical, mental or learning disabilities?

8. Do I have any individual personal or physical characteristics that set me apart from others?

9. What hobbies, activities or interests define me?

10. What are some of the roles or responsibilities that give me status?

Answering these questions will help you appreciate the full scope of diversity. Often we think of other people as different from us — physically, mentally, emotionally and genetically — when, in fact, they have the same inclinations. There are two points of view involved in diversity. Appreciating the differences and similarities establishes a means of valuing those differences.

Reflections

Reflections

An Exercise in Perspective

Diversity is an exercise in perspective and has been challenging people with its different faces since the beginning of time. Whenever more than two people have gotten together, conflicts have centered around differences, first physical, then philosophical. Brother against brother, children against parents, family against community, village against village, villages against a country, countries against countries. Leon Uris explained this incomprehensible, yet almost fatalistic, manner of discrimination in his book, *The Haj*.

People discriminated against each other based on how they saw the world: flat versus round, whether they believed the sun or earth was at the center of their universe. These egocentric points of view help explain how personal and cultural perspectives filter our opinions. We each define truth based on our familial and cultural point of view. When we consider people, customs or behaviors that are hard for us to accept, it is the degree of difference from our own point of view that causes the conflict and angst.

Prejudice and Discrimination

Every person exhibits some kind of prejudice. The dictionary defines prejudice as "an irrational attitude of hostility directed against an individual, a group, a race or their supposed characteristics." It is also defined as "a mental inclination, a preference for or disposition to something." Prejudice results in a tendency to see people who are different as being inferior in some way, to find a different point of view as less intelligent or effective. Though neither positive nor negative, the term prejudice is linked to avoidance or dislike.

Prejudice consists of the following three main elements:

1. Stereotyping. This is an almost lazy way of thinking. Rather than distinguishing differences, we lump people, things or ideas together based on the characteristics or behavior of a few. We attribute to the many what may be relevant to the few. It happens when we categorize people simply because of the way they look, dress or speak.

2. Devaluation. We make something or someone less than what they are because of an opinion. Because of a difference, we perceive them or it as inferior.

3. Authority. Rather than think for ourselves and form our own interpretations, and perhaps out of fear of being held responsible or seen as wrong, we defer to someone else. We accept what people in positions of authority tell us — a parent, a teacher or a political or religious figure.

Prejudice toward another is as unintelligent as prejudice to an untasted food. It is an unconscious acceptance of a thought. It leads to discrimination, to a specific behavior or action taken against an individual or group of people who are somehow different. In the past, prejudice in the U.S. — expressed as slavery or segregation — was much more public and obvious. Today, it can be more hidden and subtle, such as painting a swastika on one's hand or telling ethnic and sexist jokes.

South African Archbishop Desmond Tutu has been quoted as saying, "By dehumanizing and devaluing others, you are dehumanized and devalued in the process." It's easy to hate someone because they're different, especially when you don't know them, or you haven't seen them do things, value things or care about things as you do. Prejudice centers itself in an absence of fact and analysis.

Seeing Similarities

If you're like most people, making snap judgments about others is almost second nature. This is especially the case in America where we value a culture that is seen as masculine, decisive and fast to act. We tend to associate with people who are most like us. As a result, society has in the past had trouble valuing differences, which then leads to discrimination. For example, women in law enforcement and men in nursing have at times found it hard to be accepted in professions historically reserved for members of the opposite sex. It is a case of numbers: When a field is dominated by a particular majority, the field becomes defined by that majority.

Consider the last time you went to a business meeting or seminar and didn't know anyone there. Everything was okay until the breaks, when you had to make conversation with complete strangers. Then you found out that the person next to you grew up in the same city and even knew some of your old favorite high school hangouts. You continued the conversation, sat together for the rest of the afternoon and exchanged business cards. Why? Because, as the old adage goes, opposites attract? Of course not! Your similarities served as the springboard to a relationship. Your similarities bridged differences and provided a means of interpreting who she was and defined the situation.

Sizing Up People

Diversity awareness focuses on seeing difference as okay rather than a threat or something that can cause discomfort. This new awareness requires you to exercise your mind and develop new thinking patterns. For instance, when you meet someone new, you make an initial judgment in less than 30 seconds! And when you talk with someone new on the telephone, you form an opinion of that person in less than 13 seconds! For most, it's simply easier to make sweeping, instant judgments about people's intelligence, productivity, competence, honesty and more.

Typically you size up people based on the fact that they look like, act like or sound like someone you've known in the past. To rid yourself of this tendency, try following these six steps:

1. Make your initial contact with the new person.

2. Collect information.

3. Separate the facts from your opinions, theories, conjectures and suppositions.

4. Make a judgment based on only the facts.

5. Refine your judgment by periodically updating the facts.

6. Continue to expand your opinion of a person's true potential.

You can stop prejudicial thinking by challenging assumptions. Rather than accept the first thought that floats into your head, consciously size up the person yourself. Learning to thoughtfully and systematically size up someone results in more accurate, fact-based judgments and fewer stereotypes. Move out of the ruts and into a reasonable approach.

Hard as it is to deal with all the changes in the workplace and the explosion of knowledge, you must stop looking for an easy answer. Facts: People are individuals, not everyone in the engineering department wears pocket protectors and nerdy glasses, not everyone in environmental services speaks a foreign language. There are women who excel in sports and men who appreciate home decorating. Skills, talents and aptitudes blend far more now than when people were pouring off the ship onto Ellis Island. People in Europe enjoy the same games as do those in America, those in the Middle East enjoy the same music as people in the West, sporting events are attended by people of widely different ages, and more and more people realize they all share a common dream.

Seeing the other side of diversity and experiencing what others perceive can allow diversity to move toward collaboration and gain.

Consider if you have personal prejudices or blind spots. Try these exercises and discover where you need to reevaluate your thinking. Be very honest with yourself. Sometimes we try to be "politically correct" when speaking out loud, yet in our minds we are much more honest with our perceptions and feelings.

Close your eyes and complete these sentences in your mind. Don't speak them out loud. What comes unbidden into your conscious?

- "In the workplace women are usually … "
- "I believe African-Americans, for the most part, are … "
- "Most older workers tend to be … "
- "In the workplace men are usually … "
- "I believe Latin Americans, for the most part, are … "
- "Most younger workers tend to be … "
- "In the workplace physically disabled people are usually … "
- "I believe Jewish Americans, for the most part, are … "
- "Most middle-aged workers tend to be … "

Here are some questions to ponder.

1. Were you surprised by what you think?

2. If you had to find hard evidence to support your statements, could you?

3. Are all women, men, physically disabled people, African-Americans, Latin Americans, Jews, older workers, younger workers and middle-aged workers exactly as you perceived them?

4. Do people you know who are in a visible minority fit the stereotypes?

Reflections

The Golden Rule

As a child, your parents or influential people in your life may have told you to put yourself "in another person's shoes." This tactic probably worked when you and your best friend had a misunderstanding, and it can apply to increasing your understanding of your coworkers' feelings and sensitivities. You may be familiar with the American Indian proverb, "Do not judge a man until you have walked a mile in his moccasins."

Your family may have passed along another important lesson: Treat people as you would want them to treat you. Fine as the golden rule is, in the case of diversity it needs to be restated. Rather than doing what you would want done, you should do as you think they would want done. Face it, not everyone wants what we want.

Probably the best course of action is to keep an open mind and open lines of communication. Accept each person as an individual and treat her with dignity and respect. You can fall back on thinking of a time in your own life when you felt different from everyone else. Maybe it happened at school when you were the only one in class who didn't wear whatever was designated as the "in thing" to wear. Or maybe a trip overseas plunged you into a world where nobody spoke your language. Recalling personal situations like these can help you develop empathy for what others face on a daily basis.

The best tip for addressing diversity: Ask that person how she would like to be treated. Step outside your comfort zone. Be honest in trying to overcome a multitude of multicultural barriers. For example, you might say this to a physically disabled coworker:

"I'm never sure if I should open the door for you or not. I want to be helpful, but I don't want to offend you, either. What are you most comfortable with?" (This also can be an issue for men and women together in the workplace.)

Practice putting yourself "in another person's shoes." Imagine yourself in the following situations. Write a couple of sentences about the feelings and sensitivities you might experience if this were you.

- Imagine yourself as a new immigrant to the U.S.

- Imagine yourself speaking only broken English.

- Imagine yourself as a member of a different race.

- Imagine yourself as having a different religious or cultural background.

- If you're a man, imagine what it's like to be pregnant.

- Imagine yourself 25 years older or younger.

- Imagine what it's like to be confined to a wheelchair.

- How would you react to thinning or no hair?

- What would it be like to be poor?

- How would you react in a group where jokes about ethnicity were bantered about?

- Imagine yourself recently divorced in the middle of a group of married people discussing a future event.

- What would it be like to see younger people joining an organization and to worry that you were seen as dated?

- Imagine trying to appear knowledgeable about a technology everyone is discussing easily and you haven't a clue.

- Imagine not seeing clearly, not hearing well, not walking easily.

Touchy Situations

Derogatory terms used to describe people of specific ethnic, religious or racial groups are, for the most part, not condoned by society any longer. Certainly, they are not sanctioned in public. Privately, however, they continue to be uttered by some who are either ignorant or intolerant of people different from themselves. Examples we can site are the terms "girl," which can offend women, or "boy," which can offend men because of its implication.

Following are inappropriate salutations in the workplace:

- Dear
- Honey
- Mom or Pops
- Fella or Guy
- Mac
- Ace
- Sweetheart
- Babe
- Kid

The best action is to call people by their names. In most companies today, people (even top-level executives) prefer their first names. If someone's name preference is unknown or the pronunciation is unclear, ask. Assume a friendly greeting can be as intrusive as the above-mentioned generic salutations.

There are also phrases or sayings that don't seem obviously derogatory, but that certain groups still find offensive. Remarks about Irish or Scottish or Italian stereotypes may seem like harmless jokes but are not so amusing to those who feel put down by them. Avoid any slang or jargon that can appear to be a putdown.

Diversity issues surface in organizations ubiquitously, as inoffensive attempts at horseplay, or as a means to relieve stress, or to make the workplace fun or enjoyable. "Can't you take a joke?" is often a sign of this side of diversity. Intentional or not, it discriminates. It makes light of another's feelings or beliefs. The only way to come together in a supportive, collaborative environment is by recognizing the differences and uniqueness of others while appreciating the same feelings and emotions as you experience.

Read the following three scenarios, which describe an incident when someone said something inappropriate at work. After reading each scenario, ask yourself the questions on the next page.

- Scenario One: You are involved in a casual group conversation when a coworker joins your group and starts complaining that she got stuck with the "new guy," a person of color. She makes negative references to the "new guy's" intelligence and work habits and complains about the extra work that it will cost her. Some in the group laugh, while others appear embarrassed.

- Scenario Two: During lunch, a small group of employees begins speaking in a foreign language. One of your lunchmates grimaces, points to the other table and announces loudly, "You know what's really wrong with this country? Some people refuse to accept the fact that this IS America."

- Scenario Three: While waiting for a meeting to start, someone in your group tells an ethnic joke. Amid the general laughter you notice the face of a coworker whose culture has just been slandered. She is noticeably hurt. Finally, there's an awkward silence until someone else asks about a basketball score.

Reflections

Questions

- Would you object to what was said?

- If you objected, how would others react?

- If someone else objected, how would you feel or further respond?

- How might your associates feel or further respond?

- Might you or the other person be accused of being too touchy or a "poor sport" for speaking up?

- How could this incident affect your relationships with the other people present?

- If you could, how would you change the incident?

- How would you handle a similar incident in the future?

- If you or no one else spoke up, would you wish you had?

- Does this ever happen at your workplace?

Chapter 2 Summary

Every person exhibits some kind of prejudice. Former President George H. W. Bush was prejudiced against broccoli. The dictionary defines prejudice as "biased thinking; an irrational attitude of hostility directed against an individual, a group, a race or their supposed characteristics." It consists of three main elements: stereotyping, devaluation and believing what people in positions of authority tell us. Prejudice leads to discrimination, which refers to a specific behavior or action taken against an individual or group of people who are somehow different.

Because we tend to associate with people who are most like us, we often have trouble valuing differences, and this can lead to discrimination.

Diversity awareness focuses on seeing differences as normal rather than a threat or something that should cause discomfort. Instead of sizing up people based on how they look, act or sound, see people for who they are.

As a child, influential people may have told you to put yourself "in another person's shoes" and to treat other people as you would want them to treat you. The golden rule is an excellent adage for diversity appreciation, but even better, adjust it: Treat others as they would like to be treated. By being open, friendly and honest, a multitude of multicultural barriers are overcome. Ask people what they want. Accept each person as an individual and treat her with dignity and respect.

Derogatory terms used to describe people of specific ethnic, religious or racial groups or salutations that demean are inappropriate. Call people by their own names.

Inappropriate humor in the workplace causes discomfort and hurt feelings. Individuals must take responsibility for putting a stop to these inappropriate comments and jokes, especially because they can affect employee morale, job performance, productivity and, ultimately, your company's bottom line. Touchy situations, biases and unquestioned beliefs all strengthen the barriers that keep people from appreciating their differences.

Biology and culture, which make people different, are less important than how we see and react to differences. Sensitivity and respect allow us to realize, appreciate and overcome the complexities.

3 TYPES OF DIVERSITY

When most people hear the word "diversity," they think of racial differences: Caucasians, African-Americans, Latin and Hispanic Americans, Asian-Americans, American Indians, Americans from the Middle East, and more. Diversity also implies sexual harassment issues and gay rights in today's changing society. It runs deep, touching every part of our lives — from the workplace to our homes, neighborhoods, schools and places of worship; it encompasses financial and social status, education and recreation.

This handbook focuses on the workplace. In this context, there are many different ways to characterize individual workers. First, they can be categorized according to

- Seniority

- Experience

- Position or level

- Amount of education

- Amount of training

They can be characterized by whether they are

- Union

- Nonunion

- Management

- Hourly workers

- Salaried

And, they can be further categorized by

- Race

- Gender

- Age

- Sexual identity

- Personal characteristics

- Physical characteristics

- Socioeconomic status

- Social affiliations

- Religion

- Family background and culture

Diversity refers to a mixture of all these categorizations. Each characteristic and each experience make a worker unique. "Diversity awareness" occurs when we recognize all of these unique characteristics and experiences and realize that workers are more valuable because of them. Collectively, these diverse characteristics and experiences expand an organization's or team's base of knowledge and make it stronger and more effective.

The bottom line? A diverse workforce is good for business. Think of diversity as an equation like this: a person plus his personality and particular situation in a particular place and time contribute uniquely to the larger picture. Differences bring about innovation.

Seniority and Experience

A person's work life used to go something like this: You graduated from high school, trade school or perhaps college and then were hired by a company. You stayed there for the rest of your working career, either moving up the ladder through promotions or finding a comfortable niche or position to wait it out until retirement. In other words, you were a "lifer." You never considered or wanted to look elsewhere for a job. The company took care of you, and you were loyal to the company. This career practice went on for years. It became a real cause of pain and despair during the huge layoffs and reorganizations of the early '90s. People with 20 to 30 years' seniority felt betrayed, not knowing what to do next, because they were "cast aside." Career-transition consultants flourished during this massive corporate restructuring time, trying to assist people moving from one career to the next.

The mentality of one life, one career, definitely became antiquated in the mid-1970s, though there were still large portions of a generation that clung to it. By the '70s, people were experiencing an average of three to five careers in their lives. By the '90s, they were experiencing, or were told to prepare for, five to 12 different careers on average.

Again, we see times changing exponentially! Today's workforce is much more mobile and transient. People today expect to move between careers and among jobs. In fact, a popular definition is "portfolio employees." College counselors and career coaches are teaching people how to build portfolios, literally having jobs serve as examples of skill sets. Rather than use resumes to get them in a job, people use jobs to build their resumes. Workers are willing to move up, move in or move out as business needs and their own individual interests change. They see a job as a means to a life, as a step toward a goal, and not the end destination.

The massive reorganizations, restructuring, layoffs and downsizing took away any ability to see an organization as benign or a caregiver. By 1993, it was hard to find someone who hadn't experienced or known on a personal level someone who suffered from displacement. Whether willing or not, people reevaluated the benefits of "seniority." Experiences, plural, were the tickets for success. As a result of the past millennium, people with vastly different work experiences, career paths and lengths of service are now constantly brought together in the workplace. They come from different cultures and statuses.

Take, for example, the company that needs to hire a new manufacturing manager. Upper management decides that all of the internal candidates who could be promoted lack one important requirement: an "outside perspective." So the top brass chooses a young man with manufacturing management experience from a smaller company for the position. The new manager brings new ideas from his old job that boost productivity and profitability immediately. However, he also faces some resentment and lack of cooperation from the line workers who believe that one of their own should have gotten the job. In this case, the company needs to communicate and reinforce the idea that diversity in seniority and work experience benefits everyone. A couple of tactics might include posting daily manufacturing productivity and profitability reports in the break room and holding monthly meetings to recognize all workers' efforts. This type of diversity butts heads with generational differences. Teaching people the value of experience, however, allows all to benefit.

Levels: Education and Training

In small businesses, there are generally two levels of people: the owner or boss and everyone else. In large companies up until the mid-'90s, there were often many layers of managers and workers, both union and nonunion. Following the downsizing of the '90s, many companies drastically cut out layers within organizations and valiantly tried pushing down decision making. Reduced levels or tiers of employees are a reality, but there remain several layers from front-line workers to chief operating officers.

Years ago, workers at the bottom rungs of the corporate ladder rarely saw or had a chance to interact with workers on the upper rungs of the corporate ladder. And when they did, these upper-level managers were always addressed as "Mr. Jones" or "Mrs. Smith." There is the old management joke about the employee who, in his first week on the job, went to the president with what would have been a million-dollar idea. The president, instead of listening, berated the employee for his lack of awareness of how things were done and noted that in a year or two he could come talk to the president. The employee left for the competition within a short time, taking his million-dollar idea with him. Lack of acceptance such as this continues to have a devastating impact on the bottom line.

Today's corporate culture is much more relaxed. Management layers are as trim as the workforce. Instead of using titles that categorize employees, many companies refer to all of their workers — regardless of position or salary — as "associates." And everyone — including the CEO or president — is called by his first name. These changes have helped to erase some of the status consciousness in corporate America that has been recognized as a creative drain.

Relationships between unions and the companies they're affiliated with also have changed over the years. Instead of the traditional "us vs. them" adversarial relationships, many unions and companies now work together to face their business challenges. In some cases, union workers, such as those in various airlines, have accepted wage and benefit cuts in order to improve their companies' financial outlook. Instead of differences being underscored, these employees seek partnering.

Education and training are two other ways workers are differentiated. While the other differences — levels, seniority, etc. — have narrowed, diversity in knowledge and skill acquisition has remained, and in many cases continues to expand. More and more, we hear of the great chasm dividing the haves from the have-nots; educational differences in our communities are frightening to those who see basic skills like grammar and math at low levels in the workforce. The divide is even greater in the area of technology.

Some workers have college degrees, others have been trained at a technical or vocational school or even on the job, and many have high school diplomas or the equivalent. Because learning is acquired in different ways, it adds to the diversity of the workforce. Strengths as well as weaknesses are apparent, and a mix of educational levels is a notable plus.

For instance, education and training may influence the way workers view a problem. A worker with training and experience in accounting may see a big increase in the company's shipping and receiving budget as a "financial problem" and call for budget cuts. At the same time, someone with manufacturing training and experience may see it as a "procedural problem" and suggest that more efficiency be built into shipping and receiving procedures. Another worker might see it as a signal that orders are increasing, thus profitability. If these workers take the time to share their experiences and ideas, they may come up with a balanced solution to the shipping and receiving problem — trimming the budget while improving efficiency. It's a good example of how diverse knowledge and opinions often lead to the best results.

Race, Gender, Age and Sexual Identity

Race is a subgroup of people who have a combination of physical, genetic-based characteristics that distinguish them from other subgroups of people. In U.S. government reports, four racial categories are listed, along with a default category labeled "other." These categories are as follows:

- American Indian or Alaskan native

- Asian or Pacific Islander

- Black

- White

- Other

To complicate matters, the U.S. Census Bureau views race and ethnicity as two different characteristics. For example, "Hispanic" is viewed as a cultural background and not a race. Although some Hispanics can trace their ancestry to American Indians or Europeans, many would prefer to be racially identified as Hispanics. They see themselves as neither "black" nor "white." Frustration over the current racial categories increases as the U.S. continues to become more diverse and people take pride in their differences.

The way the U.S. government divides people into racial categories often leaves those from other parts of the world scratching their heads too. For instance, Caucasians are actually people who live in the Caucasus region, located between the Black and Caspian Seas. Ironically, many of these Caucasians have dark skin, a direct contrast to the American definition of Caucasian. Preconceived notions about how people think and act based on their race, gender, age and sexual preference work against diversity. While these notions emphasize the differences, the emphasis is negative and inaccurate on individual levels.

Personal Skills

When you look at yourself, your peers, your managers or the employees of an organization, you usually see personal characteristics, habits and work styles that make each of you unique. The corporate world often refers to these as "soft" skills. Here are some examples:

- Time management (being on time for work, always meeting deadlines)

- Organizational skills (ability to handle paperwork, electronic messages, scheduling and work priorities)

- Juggling or the ability to manage a variety of tasks at the same time

- Comfort with constant change in the business world

- People skills or the ability to get along with others

- Verbal and written communication skills

- Leadership skills

Not every person excels in every one of these soft-skill categories. However, you'll find people who excel in each category in most work groups. Collectively, they make a stronger team. None of the categories is associated with any race, gender, age or sexual preference.

Social and Economic Status

How, when, where and with whom we socialize makes us different and affects our behavior at work. Social affiliations include civic or political groups (chambers of commerce, Rotary, Toastmasters, Young Republicans, etc.), recreational pursuits (health clubs, sports teams, hobby groups), education and religious activities, and even our circle of friends. A worker who's always been active in sports may set the best example of how to be a team player, while someone who's a member of Toastmasters may be perfect for making a sales presentation.

Being aware of people's social affiliations can help you take advantage of their work-related strengths as well as minimize conflict in the workplace. Perhaps an employee is a member of an organization promoting women's rights. This individual could contribute great insight in selling to a client whose workforce is predominantly female. Misreading the employee's beliefs or assuming certain political positions could result in aggressive behaviors. Again, the solution is valuing the different talents, strengths and interests, and withholding judgment is what allows a team to benefit from all members.

Economic status differences are another type of diversity. Discussions about money can be heated when coworkers come from different economic backgrounds. Misunderstandings can minimize the value of these different perspectives. Topics that can benefit from different economic-status insights include:

- What salary ranges should be

- Whether to pay overtime or give comp time

- How budget dollars should be divided

- Which benefits are more valuable to the workforce

Consider the example of a company Christmas party where dressy attire is required. Because of accident liabilities, management decides not to serve liquor at company expense but instead allows employees to buy drinks at a cash bar. Some workers may think the drink prices are high and are annoyed that they had to buy new dresses or suits for the party. Perhaps management didn't anticipate these feelings when planning the party. Another diversity complication is introduced by calling it a "Christmas" party, alienating those who don't celebrate this holiday and don't show up as a result. A company function intended to be fun and bring employees closer together actually ends up dividing them. The lesson to be learned here: Let a diverse group of employees plan company-wide functions and be sure the group takes every type of diversity into consideration.

Religion, Family and Culture

It has long been counseled that there are two topics to avoid on the job: politics and religion. (The exception: If you work as a political consultant or in a religious organization.) Historically there are strong feelings about both; wise counsel is to avoid discussions on either. There are occasions when employees will want a day off to observe religious or cultural holidays. One way to handle these requests is by offering personal days or floating holidays. The City of Los Angeles is an example of an organization that plans for and around every group's important events and holidays. They prepare a calendar noting every significant date. The training department, responsible for the city's 20,000+ workforce, avoids scheduling any activity on or after any designated day. Another consideration is to avoid workplace decorations that symbolize one particular type of religion or culture.

Workers from different cultures have different values that they project on the job. For example, some people from a traditional Asian culture might have been taught to show great respect for their managers and especially for people who are older than them. In contrast, some people from another culture may see older workers as on their way to retirement with no interest in learning new high-tech skills. Again, judging an individual based on a cultural generalization can be detrimental to decision making.

It is easy to see how experiences as a child can have a big impact on later work life. Popular television shows of the 1950s and '60s seldom showed members of minority groups and more likely promoted stereotypical thinking.

Series like "Father Knows Best" and "Leave It to Beaver" reflected the ideal family: a working father, stay-at-home mother and their biological children all living under the same roof. In "I Love Lucy," Ricky's welcome upon entering the apartment was "Lucy, I'm home," further reinforcing clichéd roles. Today there is no "typical" or "ideal" family. In fact, some shows — MTV or "Beavis and Butthead" — further add to the belief that generalization is poor at best: Seriously, who wants to be like Butthead? Family life has changed drastically between 1970 and the new century, according to the U.S. Census Bureau. In the last census of the past century, a "typical" family defied quantification; there were 17 different categories of "family" from which to choose. Some changes noted in the last century include the following:

Description	1970	2000
Families headed by a married couple	87%	74%
Households with married couples and children	40%	21%
Households with married couples and no children	30.3%	33.9%
Households with people living alone	1 in 6	1 in 3
Families headed by women with no husband	5.6 million	13.2 million
Families headed by men with no wife	1.2 million	3.2 million

The most striking statistics from these comparisons are the tremendous jumps in the number of families headed by single parents or primary guardians. The number of female heads of household more than doubled, and the number of single males with children almost tripled. The category also includes families headed by a grandparent. Further explaining these changes is the choice made by many to begin a family without a partner or through artificial means. It's critical that the workplace reflects these changes in family life by offering benefits, such as flexible scheduling and on-site day care, to accommodate the needs of diverse groups of workers.

Cultural differences aren't limited to people from different countries. There are many regional differences within the United States. For example, a New

York lifestyle is seen as very different from a Southern lifestyle. A fast-talking and direct communication style common to one industry standard may seem brash to someone from a different organization. Similarly, a speech mannerism may seem unbearably slow and countrified to someone who speaks more quickly. And the casual communication style common in some regions may seem impolite to someone from a conservative area. But to generalize about a whole group or to surmise a skill or lack thereof due to a regional characteristic downplays the value of diversity.

A Balancing Act

The lesson to be learned from this discussion of diversity: There's no universal way to define diversity. There are many ways to characterize people. To group them, however, whether for ease of explanation or for lack of wisdom, is misleading if not absolutely false. As the world continues to shrink and as knowledge moves around it faster than ever with the Internet, people within each group become less similar and more individualistic. Generalizations are fraught with inaccuracy. The Southern male just doesn't look much different from the Western male anymore, and the tennis player, male or female, acts the same on the court. Referring back to the introduction of this book, the very reasons for diversity — interconnectivity, globalization and technology — minimize them on a group level. Yes, people are different, but they are different within any group in which they find themselves. Working in a culturally diverse workforce requires a delicate balancing act. Some techniques to ensure the benefits of diversity:

- Observe employees' behaviors and their cultural differences.

- Check on employees' progress periodically. Pinpoint any problems early on and address them immediately.

- Don't try to imitate another person's culture or pretend that it's understood. This is ignorance that leads to disaster down the road. Ask questions.

- Apologize at the first sign of a misinterpretation. Learn from mistakes and then move forward.

- Spread the word. Pass along new knowledge about cultural diversity to others in the company.

- Act as a role model for others when it comes to cultural awareness, sensitivity and training.

- Create a comfortable work environment for all associates and make them feel valuable to the company.

When individuals don't understand all aspects of an employee's diverse background, it can result in a host of work-related problems. These problems can affect the morale and productivity of the individual and, ultimately, the entire company or organization. To properly manage diversity, take responsibility. Become aware of it. Recognize these differences, understand them and finally blend them, making a pleasant and productive workplace for everyone.

As Joe Gilliam, author of *The Winner in You*, puts it: "People are not difficult, they are different."

Make the most of these differences.

To better understand the types of diversity, consider your own unique differences. We often think of others as different from us. Reflect on the following most common ways that people differ by finishing the phrases with what first comes to your mind.

The culture in which we were raised teaches us how to be feminine or masculine. This in turn causes us to be treated in certain ways.

A real man is

_____

_____

A real woman is

_____

_____

Race plays a big part in how we think and act and experience things.

My race is _____

I share the following characteristics with my race:

_____

_____

We define ourselves as citizens of a certain country and as people with a broad, common heritage of culture, belief and language.

My nationality is_____

We believe that

_____

_____

Reflections

The family plays a role in how we are different, with its own traditions, customs and rituals.

At our house, our customs include

_____

_____

The generation we grow up in shares experiences and shapes our thoughts.

In my generation, we

_____

_____

We make distinctions about others and ourselves on the basis of where we live and where we grew up.

Where I was raised, people are

_____

_____

We see ourselves as different based on our education, experiences and financial status.

I see myself as unique in this regard because

_____

_____

Reflections

There are different groups and levels in my organization and each interprets work differently.

In my work group, I see the people in the organization as

_____

_____

Through working together within a department, a company or an industry, we take on a corporate culture, or way of seeing things.

My organization is unique in that

_____

_____

Our religious beliefs and our philosophy about life and living shape us. We can be grouped by our faith, personal convictions or values.

I believe in several things

_____

_____

Review what you wrote and note a benefit from being in a particular group.

Reflections

Chapter 3 Summary

There are many different ways to characterize individual workers. Diversity refers to a mixture of all these characteristics. Think of diversity as an equation: Person + Personality + Situation + Place and Time = The "Big Picture" about who and what a person is and brings to a workgroup.

Diversity teaches that there's no universal way to work with all people. Here's some advice to keep in mind.

- Observe employees' behaviors and their cultural differences.

- Check on employees' progress periodically.

- Don't try to imitate another person's culture or pretend it's understood, and don't be afraid to ask questions.

- Apologize at the first sign of a misinterpretation.

- Pass along acquired knowledge about cultural diversity to others in your company.

- Act as a role model for others when it comes to cultural awareness, sensitivity and training.

- Create a comfortable work environment for all workers and make them feel valuable to your company.

To benefit from diversity, you must first be aware of it. Then you must recognize differences, understand them and finally blend them to make a pleasant and productive workplace. It isn't the company's job, or the boss's job, or the team leader's job. It is your responsibility. In discussing the types of diversity and one's responsibility, it is nice to remember a quote: "If not me, who; if not here, where; if not now, when."

4 MULTICULTURAL DIVERSITY

Perhaps the biggest area of diversity is multiculturalism. In terms of sheer volume — of types and categories, implications and assumptions, misunderstandings and generalizations — this area encompasses everyone, grouping them within cultural distinctions.

Multiculturalism is broad because it concerns the idiosyncrasies and characteristics that make up who someone is because of their heritage. America is as much a melting pot today as it was in the time of our ancestors. In fact, the workplace today reflects the multiple cultures that make up America. Because of this mix, conflicts easily arise.

What Culture Is

The dictionary defines culture as the characteristic features of a stage of civilization or the ideas and customs of a particular group in a particular period. Any group — whether ethnic or civic, organizational or social — has a culture. Culture guides our everyday behavior and tells us how to interpret others' actions. It helps us deal with life's problems and interact socially, by showing us what to do in situations, from when to make eye contact and how close to stand, to how to address someone or how to react to something. It even directs how we express emotions — how we express pain or demonstrate joy, how we view suffering or reflect caring. Culture defines the acceptable behavioral norms by which its people act.

The difficulties in a multicultural environment are caused by the variety of norms — the multiple shoulds and should-nots — that are at odds. With so many different signals and judgments in play, the risk of misunderstanding and miscommunication is high. Conflicts abound, and building rapport and trust, essential for relationships, is difficult. Add to this the fact that cultures are not static; they are constantly evolving.

There are realities about culture that complicate diversity and inclusion.

1. Culture is not overt. It is pervasive yet subtle. Cultural rules are generally not spoken and are discussed only when broken. People operate within their cultural confines in an unconscious mode, seldom questioning until faced with people who have a different set of norms, assumptions and behaviors.

2. We are essentially ethnocentric beings. Each culture today sees its norms, traditions, values and beliefs as central and accurate. We see and judge behavior from our point of view. We give labels to actions deemed negative: Loud people are aggressive, tardiness is rude, and name-droppers are deceitful. We judge based on our rules.

3. We instinctively interpret others' behaviors. When with another person, we don't just see what they are doing, but we interpret it in terms of meaning and intent. If someone bumps us and doesn't excuse herself, we think her rude. Yet in other cultures, with large populations and limited space, people are bumped by strangers, and it is neither rude nor does it require a comment. If people don't say please and thank you, we define them as lacking manners. Yet it is the Western culture that dictates a need to articulate those words.

4. We are unaware when we offend another, because we are focusing on our own meanings and rules. Joking around with someone from an Eastern culture can be seen as lacking respect. Calling an immigrant by her first name could be seen as demeaning and condescending. Arriving at 1:05 p.m. for a 1:00 p.m. meeting could be considered rude by a time-conscious executive.

5. Knowledge and awareness increase the ability to benefit from diversity. The more we can recognize different cultures and subcultures and distinguish their differences, the easier it is to respect, adhere to or discuss different interpretations.

6. Where to start is within ourselves. Recognize our own culture, our own biases, assumptions and value system. Then challenge ourselves to understand why we think and act that way, and what makes it right or wrong. Once we study the many influences that make up how we think and react to people, we can capitalize on diversity.

As you begin to understand the effects your particular culture has had on you, you can more easily distinguish other cultures. Review the statements below and check those that describe how you do things.

_____ I am aware of other cultures and regularly listen to others explain how their cultures work and how mine affects them.

_____ I realize that people of other cultures have fresh ideas and different perspectives to bring to my life and organization.

_____ I tell others how to succeed in my culture, telling them the unwritten rules and what they should know to get along.

_____ I am aware of my own peculiarities and know how people of other cultures perceive me.

_____ I recognize that when under pressure I revert to narrower beliefs about what is right and wrong.

_____ I resist the temptation to make other cultures the butt of jokes or to use generalizations and stereotypes to characterize or explain an action.

When I think of other cultures and subcultures, those that come to my mind include:

Reflections

Differences Within Cultures

There are several characteristics within each culture that are interpreted very differently. These in turn are some of the major causes of conflict and misinterpretation. Values, beliefs and attitudes differ among cultures and result in very different behaviors and interpretations. While it is easier to explain meaning by using specific groups and nationalities as points of illustration, it must be remembered as you continue reading that the following explanations are often generalizations and there are exceptions for every ethnic group. Likewise there are groups of people throughout the world who represent many of the characteristics, regardless of their ancestry. The latter, in fact, represent one major aspect of culture — that it is passed down and shared by groups working or living together.

Culture dictates religious beliefs and behaviors. It fosters values such as what is perceived as having status. Working with one's hands is honest work for some and demeaning to others. Upward mobility comes from achievement and skill in some cultures and from seniority and connections in others. Work itself is valued as a means toward an end in some cultures and the end itself in others. Some additional differences include:

- Space

  How close we stand to another person, how much and when we touch another person, and how familiar we are with them reflects culture. Western cultures traditionally prefer an arm's length, while Eastern cultures, as well as many minority cultures (Italians, Hispanics, African-Americans, for example) don't feel an invasion with a closer presence.

  A bone-crunching handshake, may be culturally preferred in the United States, but in Asia the soft handshake with the left hand brought under the clasped right hands is a sign of warmth and friendship.

  How we act in our space differs. Formality varies also among cultures. Speaking out in a meeting in America is accepted while offhand comments in a meeting in Korea or Japan are not appreciated. Talking about personal matters can also be interpreted by different cultures as discourteous, and getting things off the chest may not be valued as a benefit.

Introductions, how we come together, are more formal in the East than the West. First and last names are used, titles are included, and posture is more erect. Many cultures distinguish formality by having in their language two forms of the word "you," one formal and one more familiar for family, friends and children. This is seen in the French, Spanish and Italian languages, for example.

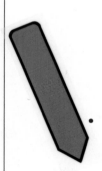

- Time

North America is very time-conscious, whereas time is perceived in a much larger context in the Middle East. We see time as a commodity, trying to save it, using it as a measure of effectiveness and defining others by their adherence to it.

Likewise people of status are seen as able to violate and manipulate time — professors, managers and owners can arrive late or complete things as they wish. Other cultures value time in a much greater perspective, falling back on their history and the very passage of time which defines their people.

- Communication and language

Even though English is becoming the business language of the world, we must recognize that communication goes beyond the words. Fifty to 90 percent of communication is nonverbal. Meaning is derived by tone, gestures and facial expressions. Rolled eyes, smirks or raised eyebrows convey sarcasm, skepticism or disdain. Eye contact can display attention and respect in America, yet cultures such as the American Indian or the Asian see eyes dropping as a sign of deference.

Some cultures see speaking up as a right of the elders, the boss or someone in authority. In other cultures, youth is revered and allowed more latitude.

The Western, English-speaking cultures see directness as a correct means of communication. In the Middle East and in Japanese culture, value is placed on inference and deducing meaning.

- Relationships

Family is a fundamental unit in most societies, but how it is defined is distinct. For the Italian or Hispanic or Asian, relatives are many times removed. Cultures such as these see allegiance as owed to family over outsiders in terms of jobs. The American Indian places family and elders above friendships and even marital relationships.

The English, or the American, culture sees family as an immediate relationship with people directly related. Friendships and relationships other than those based on family are valued.

- Dress and appearance

Culture dictates what is proper in terms of dress. In America we are becoming much less formal both at work and at religious occasions. This is particularly true of younger generations. If a subculture dictates that someone looks good in an outfit, however casual it is, she might very well wear it to make an impression on a job interviewer. Likewise, an important occasion like a visit to the doctor or to church might cause a Hispanic to dress in more formal clothes.

Personal hygiene is also dictated by culture. In Europe, for example, daily bathing is not a cultural norm, due to facilities and availability. In Egypt and many African countries, a nearby river serves multiple purposes, from personal washing to washing clothes and eating utensils.

- Food and eating habits

Cultures and religious beliefs differ in the types of food eaten and how food is eaten. Devout Muslims eat no pork. Jews who adhere to kosher food laws eat only food prepared according to strict guidelines. Seventh Day Adventists eat a vegetarian diet, and Roman Catholics avoid meat during specified days of fasting. Becoming aware of these preferences is a tangible sign of respect.

- Learning

  Culture dictates the value placed on learning. Immigrants have traditionally held learning and education as valuable, a means for success. Many cultures see learning as more of a life process, something that simply occurs as one moves through life.

  Thinking is culturally influenced, with some encouraging a linear, logical approach and others favoring images, and lateral and intuitive processing. Tied to this is the approach some cultures take toward what is in a person's control and what is beyond her control. In the workplace, this perspective can be seen in workers who see achievement as a result of hard work and education versus those who see their lives dictated by chance, luck or fate.

Cultural Norms at Work

Cultural differences are at the heart of many incorrectly labeled motivation problems in the workplace. Treating everyone as we want to be treated was challenged in the second chapter of this book. It doesn't work. Cultures give value to different acts. As David McClelland, Harvard psychologist, noted, "We all have needs for achievement, affiliation and status; what is different between groups of individuals is the way in which these needs are satisfied."

Oscar Wilde remarked once that it took two to speak the truth, one to listen and one to speak. We can paraphrase this to say that, in the workplace, effective communication needs one to listen, one to speak and both to understand the cultural interpretations.

There are three major differences in cultural values that should be understood.

1. First is a respect for authority. Two-thirds of all cultures respect authority. This causes people to have formal communication channels, favoring hierarchical structures and hesitating to question

or contribute ideas. Certainly respect for authority makes it rude to challenge statements and can hinder openness and trust. This attitude is being regularly condemned by the younger generation. Historically it is the youth and the educated who assign respect to knowledge rather than rank, age or status.

2. Second is assigning individual responsibility. In American business, "the buck stops here" is a well-respected message. In other cultures, group responsibility is favored. Praise and blame are collective in cultures where collaboration and harmony are more important than individual competition. Value on the "team" is high, for example, in island cultures and the Pacific Rim.

3. Third is the attitude of control over one's environment. A majority of cultures are more fatalistic than the American culture. The history of the United States explains how an internal focus of control evolved. We can "fight City Hall" and "anyone can be president." In other cultures, the will of God, Allah or a higher being is seen as the controlling factor.

Consider how these different attitudes and values can play out in your workforce.

- An excellent employee, a Native Alaskan, refuses a supervisory promotion.

- An African-American female receives a mediocre evaluation stating that others do not perceive her as a team player.

- A Thai-American female answers that she understands what the boss wants, then is observed doing something totally opposite.

- The day after a supervisor calls a top Asian-American employee into her office to point out her mistakes in an effort to correct them in the future, the employee does not come to work.

- A boss becomes angry when a Hispanic employee requests repeated days off to take his partner, who is capable of driving herself, to the doctor.

Each situation expresses cultural differences in the perception of rewards, authority and obligation. These can become detrimental when the reasons and values of the employee are not appreciated.

Ways to Work With a Multicultural Workforce

Techniques that can help you in a multicultural workplace include:

1. Ask the person. Request that the employee tell you about her cultural norms. Make this a real discussion and attempt at understanding. Some questions to probe: "What are the biggest differences between our cultures?" "What are some of the most difficult adjustments you have made in living in the United States?" "What do you wish we understood about your culture?" "What is important to you on the job?"

2. Seek out colleagues from other cultures. Ask associates and colleagues who are from the cultures represented in your work. Learn the subtle and significant cultural norms that could cause misunderstandings. Question them on what they perceive might be areas of friction.

3. Check out community resources. Determine if there are community organizations, such as the Anti-Defamation League, to learn of differences. Ethnic associations, such as the Korean Businessmen's Association, social service agencies and refugee resettlement agencies are excellent sources of information about the cultures they represent. Catholic Services and the Don Bosco Centers in major cities, for example, have evening classes on assimilation and understanding of differences.

4. Read and study about the cultures. Books available at libraries and through the Internet provide information directly. Examples include such nonfiction works as *Communicating With the Mexicans*, *Considering Filipinos*, and *How to Communicate Better With Clients, Customers and Workers Whose English Is Limited*. Fiction

works such as *Shogun*, *Tipai*, or *Love in the Time of Cholera* are also excellent tutorials on a different people.

5. Observe without judgment. Be attentive to how people behave, what they say and how they communicate and relate to each other. Notice adult-child relationships. You can see culture in action when observing a parent with a child. Americans tend to be more verbal with their children than are Mexican parents. The former will tend to verbalize directions, for example, while the latter will move close, take a hand and teach by demonstration.

6. Tell co-workers what you learn. Talk about cultural differences in staff meetings and informal gatherings. Share insights about norms and better ways for handling situations. Mentorships work well in teaching each other how to succeed with diversity.

7. Conduct focus groups. You can learn more formally by organizing culture-specific focus groups to get information through group discussions.

8. Study employee or customer surveys. Pick up information by analyzing what your customers complain about or praise. If they make comments that employees rush through a service, for example, they may be indicating the time issue. If they complain about performance reviews, they may be focusing on communication concerns or relationships. These clues can direct you to where you need to learn more.

9. Experiment with different ways to handle diversity. Trial and error can be an excellent way to improve diversity. When there is conflict between groups, try a different approach or suggest new behaviors to affect change.

10. Spend time in other cultures. Take trips, watch foreign films, visit chat rooms hosting different cultures, listen to foreign radio stations. By immersing yourself in other cultures' literature, spending time in ethnic communities and watching other-language TV stations, you can learn behaviors and norms.

Culture Goes Beyond Language

Communication is more than words and jargon. Cultures express their varied norms in nonverbal aspects, and people new to American culture may bring their own ways of speaking and acting into the workplace. This in turn may foster misunderstandings. For example, a person from India who stands close and speaks in a loud pitch could be seen as pushy. A Hispanic who drops her eyes when you address her could be seen as passive. The Japanese who appears impassive could be perceived as deceptive. The Filipina who uses pronouns interchangeably could be labeled uneducated. The Middle Easterner who visits before getting to the point is seen as not serious. The African-American who makes direct eye contact while remaining silent or the American Indian who stares could be thought to be aggressive. Each of these examples are misinterpretations of nonverbal communication.

Differences in Nonverbal Rules

The degree of directness in communication varies drastically among cultures. Americans and Northern Europeans generally see communication pragmatically, as a means of getting information across and accomplishing tasks. The majority of cultures, however, see it as a means for building relationships. In the Middle East, for example, business cannot begin — even if it is to buy a token at a souvenir store — until a cup of green tea is taken and an inconsequential conversation has occurred. Whereas this chitchat could be seen as a waste of time by American standards, where no relationship other than one-time business is desired, it is a part of the very fabric of the Arab or Israeli culture. Americans' direct "let's get to the point" approach may seem rude, cold and offensive to other cultures.

There are many topics that some cultures find offensive. Many Asian groups regard feelings as private and not to be shared. A Latino might welcome questions about the family while an Arab or Asian could find this intrusive. Discussing the price paid for something is considered ill-mannered by Western cultures while Eastern groups think nothing of it.

Behaviors learned during childhood add to the confusion. The narrowed eyes of an Asian show the same anger as the widened eyes of an American. A direct stare by an African-American or Arab does not challenge authority as does a stare during a typical meeting in corporate America. A smile and a nod could be for saving face and in no way imply agreement.

Human touch is believed to be critical to well-being. It can also be misconstrued. Devout Muslim and Orthodox Jewish men don't touch women outside their families, even to shake hands. A soft, gentle handshake meant to be polite can be taken as wimpy. Sexual harassment concerns dictate that touch be limited to the hand, elbow or top of the shoulder, yet even this type of touch may be too intimate for some cultures.

Silence as well as volume can be misinterpreted among cultures. While most Americans recognize the value of the pregnant pause, most avoid silence. Many employees in the workplace will jump right in if there is silence, whether it is during an interview or an evaluation. In Japan, however, silence is a chance for serious consideration of what has been said and is a gesture of respect to the other.

Dealing With Frustration in Multicultural Situations

When faced with misunderstanding or confusion, you will often hear someone say "speak slower" or "speak up." This can initiate a spiral of non-communication, adding frustration and often anger. When anger enters into a situation, understanding is blocked and conflict accelerates. It is important to recognize anger for what it is — frustration. If left unchecked, it can irrationally spin into a turf issue — my territory, my workplace, do it my way. Emotions enter in and issues go much deeper than whatever was initially discussed. Power and esteem come into play.

Take control, slow down the interaction and stick to the point. If frustration continues, bring in someone who can interpret what is happening.

A real hot spot for many workplaces is the speaking of languages other than English on the job. Tempers flare and the turf issue gets distorted, polarizing groups and building animosity. Reason is not involved in a situation like this; in fact, it makes no sense to become upset because a group of people who are uncomfortable or in need communicate with each other as best they can. In a foreign place, such as the Amazon, where all those around you would probably be speaking Portuguese, isn't it imaginable that you would turn to a fellow American, drop your basic Portuguese and converse in English? The place to begin appreciating diversity is to question assumptions concerning the very basics of language.

Assumptions Cause All the Problems

"Hey, they're talking about me!" "They are too lazy to learn English." "They are just being stubborn." These are a few examples of the conclusions that many jump to when they hear languages they don't comprehend. People have many reasons for their behavior, from honestly trying to improve something to working so hard to achieve that there is little time for greater adaptation. Pecking order, lack of self-esteem and ignorance are but a few reasons why we get stuck in thinking ruts. Accepting what someone else used as an explanation does not further diversity. Rethink your assumptions. Reason things out for yourself.

When faced with communicating with someone where there is limited understanding, try a few techniques like the following:

- Making things visual. Use pictures, graphs, diagrams, and symbols.

- Doing a show and tell, demonstrating what you are explaining.

- Using their language. Voice what words you know to help the situation.

- Taking it easy. Rather than panic, slow down, pause and indicate nonverbally that you are trying.

- Walking in their shoes. Realize that it is probably very painful for them also.

Appreciating what cultural shock is and realizing how different and foreign cultures can be are important steps toward valuing diversity.

Valuing diversity often requires you to literally dig yourself out of thinking ruts and apply reason to interpreting situations.

Consider which of the following statements reflect your feelings.

___ I am cognizant of what is taking place in the media and how the media affect my cultural values.

___ I find ways of using media to support important values of my culture and to learn about other cultures.

___ I am active at work trying to correct stereotypes of others.

___ I talk with others about their biases and raise awareness of fallacies.

___ I let my feelings and values be known, especially when something offends me concerning a misrepresentation of another's culture.

___ I speak up if an off-colored joke or something offensive about another is said.

___ I realize that even though some things are often repeated, saying them myself, though I don't mean offense, is not right.

___ Attributing characteristics to individuals because they are believed to represent a group or culture is detrimental to diversity.

___ Teasing someone or making a joke to lighten things up does not make what was said acceptable if it is negative about another person.

___ I understand that others' views of work and life can be different from mine.

Review the statements and reevaluate any assumptions or beliefs you might have toward various cultures.

Reflections
Reflections

Chapter 4 Summary

Progress is being made in the workplace; demographics are changing. White males no longer are the dominant culture in many workplaces. Women and minority cultures are no longer found in certain specific levels within an organization. Learning about cultures and appreciating the differences of various people enrich the workplace.

Realizing what culture is and how it affects understanding and perception is a first step in minimizing conflict and misunderstanding. Appreciate how values, beliefs and attitudes cause differences in the perception of space, time, dress, communication, eating habits and relationships.

Treating people as individuals requires that we step away from group assumptions and listen carefully to others. Notice that some people are less direct in their communication. Some topics are considered discourteous, and eye contact can signal disrespect for some people. Touch, voice tone and the allowance of silence all have different meanings for individuals.

While it is from a culture that people often develop tendencies, traits and characteristics and learn to behave in certain ways, the differences are just that — behaviors and tendencies. People have strengths and abilities that are unique and can provide variety and creativity to a workplace. Different thinking adds power to a team's effectiveness.

What doesn't help is responding to misunderstandings with anger. What does help is understanding. Study after study indicates that the more educated and knowledgeable one is, the more tolerance she displays. Learn about, read about, and immerse yourself in other cultures so that you can gain from the differences that diversity brings to a workplace. Turn the potential conflicts into strong collaboration.

5 CONFLICT AMONG GENERATIONS

Multiculturalism may be the biggest area of diversity, but age is increasingly seen as the most volatile in terms of misunderstanding. At no other time in history have four generations worked side by side in an organization. Each generation has different worldviews, values and attitudes. There are generational personalities, with different preferences for doing work, listening to music, and using free time. And, there is conflict.

The generations can't even arrive at a definition for old age. Depending on whom you ask, it could be anyone over 30; however, the Bureau of Labor Statistics says it's 55 and the Census Bureau says it's 65.

What is not under debate is the aging of the workforce. Statistically speaking, over half of all Americans are older than 45 and those over 50 are increasing in numbers. An increasing challenge for future generations is the care of retired workers. A challenge within the workplace is whether they will retire! People are staying on the job longer — retiring later and living longer.

A Time/CNN poll taken in 1998 revealed that 24 percent of respondents supported the idea of raising the retirement age while still retaining full social security benefits.

Ageism

Discrimination based on age is known as ageism. The Age Discrimination Employment Act (ADEA) of 1976 protects employees between the ages of 40 and 70 from workplace discrimination and covers government and all private companies with at least 20 employees, as well as labor unions and employment agencies.

Specifically, the ADEA eliminates mandatory retirement at any age for most occupations and includes employment guidelines in the following four areas:

1. Recruiting. Practices in the past discriminated against older workers with comparable credentials and more on-the-job experience. A tight job market and the need for talent minimize discrimination as much as the laws prohibit it.

2. Hiring. Companies cannot ask job applicants about their age. However, a bona fide occupation qualification (BFOQ) — typically a physical requirement — may disqualify some older persons from certain jobs. Similarly, age requirements are more stringent in public-safety positions, such as police officers, firefighters and air traffic controllers.

3. Promotions. More lawsuits are filed over promotion discrimination than anything else. Promotional decisions must be based on an objective job-performance appraisal system, keeping employees informed about their opportunities for advancement.

4. Terminations. A company cannot fire an employee because of age. If substandard performance is an issue, an older employee must be given a fair chance to improve his performance.

When organizations are faced with downsizing, termination or industry changes, they must take care concerning the over-40 employee. The laws protect workers from the possibility of lengthy unemployment, under-employment and lower wages. They can also be seen as protection for an organization so that talent and an institutional history remain. Companies that discriminate through lack of promotional or training opportunities for older employees hurt themselves. They feel they won't recoup the time and money invested in training and, therefore, don't realize the talent drain or potentially greater cost in replacement.

Misconceptions About Older Workers

Generalizations and misconceptions about age are as erroneous as those about different cultures. Stereotypical beliefs, when coupled with the whispers about older persons standing in the way of younger workers seeking better jobs, hurt teamwork and stifle collaboration.

Research on how the mind works and how the body ages continues to disprove many of the myths concerning age. A study conducted by the American Association of Retired Persons (AARP) found that 92 percent of people 65 and older who had maintained a healthy lifestyle showed no significant mental deterioration. Only 8 percent displayed symptoms such as partial memory loss and slowed reaction time. Studies on aging continue to note aptitudes that parallel aging, such as ease and speed at relearning or adapting skills and ability to increase performance speeds on certain complex, repetitive tasks.

Benefits of age diversity in the workplace focus on problem-solving and decision-making strengths and large reservoirs of experience from which to pull ideas. An ability to adapt to change is more related to personality than to age.

According to the Bureau of Labor Statistics, occupational injuries actually occur more frequently to younger workers than older ones. Some studies say that because older employees are more careful, their accident rate is less than half that of younger employees. Absenteeism is also lower with senior workers and they take fewer personal days. Younger employees take more stress-related "mental health" days or miss work because of family responsibilities. Additional benefits of age diversity include competency, years of invaluable on-the-job experience, a strong work ethic and morale, and high job satisfaction. Older workers also make great mentors for younger and less experienced workers.

The Great Age Divide

The age divide that threatens the benefits of a diverse workforce is not confined to the senior workers. As noted at the beginning of this chapter, the clash among different generations lessens what organizations can achieve. Consider various age groups as individual cultures, or subcultures within larger ones.

Dr. Morris Massey, an author on the subject of age-group "programming," says we are who we are because of the era in which we were raised. In other words, when we were born creates in us unique values, prejudices and reactions that eventually manifest themselves in the workplace. According to Dr. Massey, people who grew up during the Depression have very identifiable beliefs about money and waste. Because of the hardships they faced or witnessed, they tend to be more frugal. They save their money rather than spend it and make things like cars and furniture last as long as possible. Most have a strong work ethic and emphasize financial stability.

Those characteristics are in stark contrast to the baby boomers, who were born between 1946 and 1965. Because they grew up in an era of economic prosperity, they are often criticized for turning spending and consumption of consumer goods into an art form. While they value work, they also value play and the pursuit of leisure activities. During the 1970s, they were often referred to as the "Me Generation."

Other historians and authors have studied this phenomenon of generations and added to the findings of Massey. In addition to veterans or seniors and the boomers, there are the Generation X'ers and the nexters, though none appreciate the labels used to describe them. An excellent piece of research, *Generations at Work* by Zemke, Raines and Filipczak, more clearly notes the chasms between different workers and goes on to suggest means of benefiting from working together. The problems plaguing the workplace are not downsizing or technology, lousy bosses or corporate greed. The overriding problems are ones of values, ambitions, views and clashing mind-sets.

How Generations Differ

An individual's date of birth is a defining statistic, putting him in a cohort, or group of like people. These groups tend to share common tastes, attitudes and experiences; they are a product of their time. Such circumstances — economic, social, sociological and demographic — cause defining moments at formative stages in their lives. The adage holds that "people resemble their times more than their parents." Because generations share a time in history with common events, images and experiences, they develop their own unique personalities. These commonalities cut across racial, ethnic and economic differences. And, they bring them into the workplace.

Building on Massey's insights, the veterans were born roughly between 1922 and 1943. All but the youngest came of age around World War II and are traditionalist and the last of the gray flannel suits. They bring to the workplace "American values," civic pride, loyalty, and respect for authority, and are the classic "keepers of the grail." They clash regularly with the action-oriented boomers and the technology-focused X'ers. As assets to an organization, they are the repositories of wisdom, practical strategies and networks. They are seen as power brokers in big business, holding top executive slots and controlling significant parts of optional spending.

The baby boomers can be defined as those born between 1943 and 1969. Massey used 1946, but generational studies now note periods of "cusp," or certain years where people bridge between value sets. Those born in 1943 through 1946 have been significantly influenced by veteran values, and have been caught up in the boomer-triggering events. Postwar babies see the generational world as "pre-us," "us" and "post-us," viewing others as the problems. Boomers brought in the 60-hour workweek and are passionate about participation, involvement and quality in the workplace. They want humanity and fairness, are advocates of civil rights, empowerment and diversity. Mental and physical fitness have always been a part of their regime, and they see no reason to leave a workplace until or unless they are ready.

The X'ers entered the workplace without the joy and optimism of the boomers. Born between 1961 and 1980, they bring with them skepticism and impatience. No loyalty here, they watched parents put in long hours and still be cast aside by corporate giants. Often called latchkey children, they learned independence firsthand. Though segmented as a cohort, they share a need for flexibility and feedback, dislike close supervision, are adept with change, and are more likely to keep their own counsel and take care of #1.

They are more positive about their personal futures, and see work as a means to an end rather than the end itself, as their parents' generation did.

The nexters, born from 1980 through the millennium, are also called the millenniums. They are a nurtured, cared-for group, optimistic and respectful of what their parents think. They have easy attitudes toward gender stereotyping, are comfortable with time and space, are confused about issues of race or ethnicity, and have Internet connections throughout the world. They are willing to work and learn, leaning comfortably to the veterans' values. Confident and achievement-oriented, they move easily from fast food to grocery store carryout, yard work to Web-page construction.

Workplace Challenges

These very different generations have unique work ethics, different perspectives, preferred ways of living, idiosyncratic styles and unique views of such work-world issues as service, quality, work hours, managing and being managed. For diversity to work, it must be accepted that there is no universal approach for managing these groups. Motivation, valued benefits and ways of talking must be adjusted to each cohort and to the individuals within each. Concerns are many.

- How can project management work with senior workers and younger employees both on the same team?

- What can be done to tone down the know-it-all, moralistic older worker while getting the younger ones to stop rolling their eyes and tune in and learn?

- How can production demands be met when workers are refusing overtime and demanding that they be allowed to work the hours they were hired to work?

- Can customer service training teach tact and sensitivity to the techno-wizards who scorn their customers' lack of knowledge and hesitancy to buy what they know is superior?

- What can be done about the lax adherence to deadlines and appointments and the seemingly disrespectful approach to others' priorities?

Mixing any of these groups of workers on the job can cause clashes. For instance, the September 1998 issue of *Fast Company* points out the divide between the twentysomethings and the fortysomethings, who often look at each other with distrust, disregard and even downright dislike. From the twentysomethings' perspective, the fortysomethings just aren't "current" enough. And from the fortysomethings' perspective, the twentysomethings lack much needed experience. Bringing the generations together on the job is a diversity goal: one generation's experience coupled with the other generation's energy.

Working Together

To bridge the generation gap, one idea is to assign employees from different age groups to work together in teams and on committees. The relationships formed by working together often help in overcoming prejudices about age and other factors. Mentoring, partnering and buddy systems are excellent proactive ways to merge the generations.

A second way to benefit from diversity is to help members of each generation see how others view them and how they see other generations.

According to Zemke et al. in their research on generations at work, veterans are seen by other workers as

Boomers	Gen X'ers	Nexters
Bossy	Rigid	Trustworthy
Inhibited	Unable to get it	Great leaders
Narrow-minded	Have-alls	Fearless, strong

The Boomers are viewed as

Veterans	Gen X'ers	Nexters
Talk too much	Moralistic	Workaholics
"Me generation"	Too teachy	Great to hang with
Too soft	In the way	Focused

Generation X'ers are seen as

Veterans	Boomers	Nexters
No respect	Lazy	Too serious
No basis for critique	Know-it-alls	Driven
No value for procedure	Too techie	Critical

The Nexters are viewed as

Veterans	Boomers	Gen X'ers
Polite	Precious children	Boomer repeats
Smart	Require direction	Dimwitted
A bit soft	Need attention	Spoiled

These different perspectives identify potential mine-fields; however, the way each generation sees the world is a springboard for opportunity.

While any qualification of a group will have exceptions, generally we can anticipate that the veterans are practical, the boomers are optimistic, the X'ers are skeptical and the nexters are hopeful. In terms of work, veterans are a dedicated group, boomers for the most part are driven, X'ers are more balanced and nexters are determined. Veterans respect authority while boomers have mixed reactions toward it. X'ers give no value to authority figures, and nexters are polite.

For the veteran, hierarchy is important; to the boomer, leadership is through collectivism and group consensus; Gen X'ers are influenced by competency and nexters prefer collaboration. The groups relate to one another differently. The veterans show favor through sacrifice, the boomers through fun, the X'ers don't want closeness at work, and the nexters want to be a part of things. Demotivators include crudeness for the veterans, political incorrectness for the boomers, clichés for the X'ers and phoniness for the nexters.

The need for help with understanding each other is most evident between the boomers and the Gen X'ers. In *Revolution X* by Rob Nelson, the author noted, "We are facing an unprecedented battle between the baby boomers and everyone born after 1960. The signs pointing to such a battle are numerical, not rhetorical; they grow out of economic and social trends ... no one wants to face this kind of intergenerational tension."

The unrest and distrust brewing between the two largest groups of people in the workforce center around the self-indulgent generation on the one side and their deprived predecessors on the other.

What to Do

Experts cite several plausible actions to add enjoyment and satisfaction to the workplace. A balance can be reached. Some things to try include:

1. Get both groups to acknowledge and strive to eliminate the parent/child mind-set that is causing anger.

2. Encourage each to look at the situation from the perspective of the other and challenge subjectivity.

3. Support the boomers in getting a life and cutting down on those plus-60 workweeks so they are not so tense with their subordinates.

4. Train the boomers on delegating work and planning for the downtime so that X'ers have real work to accomplish.

5. Provide development, counseling and mentorships for X'ers so that they can more realistically plan their next career moves.

6. Help the X'ers see that they need not keep "biding" their time until the boomers retire. Focus their energies on what is happening on their jobs now.

7. Set up management training and make resources available so that the boomers learn how to let go and allow X'ers — no matter how junior — to make job decisions and direct projects on their own.

8. Talk with the entire team. Let them know the challenges and pitfalls in the economy and their own industry. Discuss their roles frankly and allow them to determine what strengths and choices they bring to the team.

The Benefits of Age and Seniority

There are many actions that an organization can take to capitalize on a diverse workforce. Allow those nearing retirement to work part time training younger workers or contract with them to complete special projects that other employees don't have the time to do. Establish a retention policy that can result in lowered pension costs, reduced employee turnover and retraining costs, improved employee morale, and an enhanced reputation for their company within the company.

Additional tips include the following:

• Get the groups together to listen to what each has to say. Gain insights from their experiences and learn more about their interests, desires and needs.

• Help them teach each other. Older workers make great mentors for younger employees.

• Aid them in developing empathy for the others' situations.

- Encourage them to keep learning. Offer them plenty of training opportunities to learn new skills, particularly computer and technology skills.

- Continue to do career planning with older employees. Keep them informed of possible changes in skill and experience requirements for certain jobs.

- Consider everyone for promotions. Don't count some out because of their age or experience. Look at the whole person — their experience, skills and abilities. If promotions aren't an option, look for lateral moves that may provide them with new career opportunities.

- Keep each generation motivated. Individualize benefits so that what employees do is relevant and valued.

- Give more flexible employment options, such as flextime, part-time, telecommuting or contract work, to all workers.

- Be aware of age discrimination and make it a part of the company's diversity training. Educate all employees about ADEA.

Forget the old adage, "You can't teach an old dog new tricks."

Today's old dogs aren't as old as they might seem. And they can be some of the best leaders for the different generations to learn how to work together.

How does your company bring employees of different generations together? Think of some ways you can strategically combine the strengths of these groups so everyone — including your company — benefits.

Idea #1:

_____

Idea #2:

_____

Idea #3:

_____

Consider the people with whom you work and jot down thoughts on their

Perspective on work:

_____

Communication style:

_____

View of authority:

_____

Reaction to approval:

_____

Work ethic:

_____

Perspective on resources:

_____

Focus:

_____

Reaction to policies and procedures:

_____

Thoughts on entitlement:

_____

Perspective of the future:

_____

What do you see as a key generational issue?

Reflections

Chapter 5 Summary

Statistically, the American workplace is aging. Discrimination based on age is known as ageism. The Age Discrimination Employment Act (ADEA) of 1976 protects employees between the ages of 40 and 70 from workplace discrimination in four main areas: recruiting, hiring, promotions and terminations. Another form of discrimination is lack of opportunities to help older workers upgrade their skills. Companies often see little or no need to train their employees over age 50 because they're nearing retirement age.

These issues come into play in such activities as recruitment, development and training, performance reviews and appraisals, counseling and terminations. They require both sensitivity and real understanding of the law.

A greater challenge to diversity is the generational clash occurring in organizations throughout America. There are four distinct groups of workers: veterans, baby boomers, Generation X'ers and nexters.

Each has vastly different perspectives on what work is and how to accomplish it. Some generations, like the boomers and the X'ers, barely get along. This not only deprives the organization of key talents, but also adds tension.

There are a variety of techniques and activities that organizations can undertake to promote diversity and appreciation of individual talents. They require that individual cohorts, or groups, learn about and empathize with the others. This requires strong leadership. With race or ethnicity, dealing with disability or some other overt difference, it is easy to see that discrimination and assumptions are wrong. With age and generational issues, though, it looks more like personality or personal squabbles. It is hard to realize that the differences are based on year of birth, how people were raised, and with whom they played.

Focus on the individual and the multiple benefits each has to offer the other.

6 GENDER, SEXUAL ORIENTATION

Gender has long been a diversity concern. Clashes occur because of differences in looks, aptitudes and communication style, as well as the sensitive problems that arise from gender issues. Alternative lifestyles, gays, transgender workers, AIDS and sexual harassment are all issues for diversity. To keep someone from contributing to her fullest because of any of the above differences is to rob the workforce of needed talent.

Different but not Equal

Title VII of the amended 1964 Civil Rights Act says that men and women must be treated equally on the job. In other words, a company can't discriminate against women when it comes to hiring, firing, pay, promotions and benefits. This law is enforced by the EEOC.

Equality continues to be questioned, especially in regard to paychecks despite the many advances. The National Committee on Pay Equity designated Thursday, April 8, 1999, as Equal Pay Day. What this meant was that a woman would have had to work from the start of 1998 to this day in 1999 in order to receive the same pay as a man who had worked only during 1998. Further evidence of pay inequity came from the president's Council of Economic Advisers, which reported that in 1998, women earned about 75 cents for every dollar earned by men. A 2000 *Fortune* magazine report showed that women with bachelor's degrees earned an average of $33,000 annually compared with $53,000 for men. The gender gap for those with graduate degrees was $43,000 for women compared to $70,000 for men. This gap was noted in fields of engineering and accounting, and occurred to women regardless of where their degrees were earned; a Cornell graduate experienced the same inequality as the state college grad.

The Glass Ceiling

The "glass ceiling," referring to the invisible barriers that keep women from advancing in an organization, may be higher today than when first defined in the late '80s. Women hit ceilings in terms of promotions, pay and opportunity. In 1990, women made up 50 percent of the workforce and held less than 3 percent of the top jobs in Fortune 500 companies. By 1996, the percentages of promotions rose and in 2000 rose again. Generational attitudes and skill needs reshape thinking. However, the numbers and the pay are still areas of concern.

Though highly qualified women have been overlooked for promotions, this is now more a case of not having a truly qualified talent pool of women in place to draw upon. As the number of women in multilevels of an organization increases, so do their talents and, thus, so does their advancement. Traditional executive ranks, comprised of white males in their 50s and 60s, are disappearing. With women and minorities entering the workplace in larger numbers than Caucasian males — some 15 million new entrants in the last decade alone — the benefit of women is evident.

In 2000, *Working Woman* magazine surveyed 1,500 minority women who worked at 17 Fortune 1000 companies. It was learned that talented females deserted the ranks of corporate America because of racism, lack of advancement opportunities, and difficulties balancing work and family responsibilities. Forty-two percent of the women admitted that they had fewer chances to be promoted when compared to men with similar qualifications and experience. Nearly one-half said they had to de-emphasize their race or ethnicity in order to succeed, and 37 percent said they had to play down their gender. Even more disturbing, 61 percent reported hearing sexist and sexual jokes, while more than half had heard racial and ethnic jokes.

When asked how a company should respond to these concerns, two-thirds of the women cited flexible scheduling. In addition, they suggested career-advancement programs, mentoring programs, and more educational and training opportunities. Of course, they should also insist on sexual harassment and sensitivity training for their insensitive co-workers.

Additional recommendations, from the Women's Bureau of the U.S. Labor Department, include the following:

- Strive for diversity among job applicants. Encourage both men and women to apply for open positions.

- Offer competitive wages for jobs for both men and women.

- Develop a system for valuing the skills and responsibilities of each position in the company so the job requirements, including training, are fairly reflected. For instance, a job that includes using several computer software packages should be more valued than a job that includes making deliveries.

- Compare pay levels among jobs that are similarly valued, specifically looking for gender-based pay gaps. Make sure that bonuses or commissions don't favor men over women.

- Analyze the way employees' performances are evaluated and raises are given. Again, treat men and women equally.

- Offer equal training and promotional opportunities to both genders.

- Assess how company promotional decisions are made. Make sure your female employees get the same opportunities for advancement as your male employees do.

- Encourage your female employees to apply for promotions.

White, Male and Worried?

One of the biggest challenges facing diversity trainers is making Caucasian males feel comfortable with the fact that they're now the minority in the American workforce. Many already feel they've suffered from "reverse discrimination." A *Newsweek* magazine cover story described this condition as "White Male Paranoia," while *BusinessWeek* titled its article "White, Male and Worried."

While the fact remains that white males still dominate the upper-management ranks and executive positions at most companies and organizations, industries like manufacturing and transportation feel the tensions on the ground level. Even an internal report issued in January 1998 by the U.S. Postal Service revealed this tendency. Federal agencies are required by law to diversify their workforce. A follow-up study by the General Accounting Office found the overall representation of women and minorities in USPS high-level management positions was almost 20 percent lower than their representation in lower-level jobs. Furthermore, although this representation increased between 1993 and 1997, the number of African-American men in upper-level jobs actually decreased during the same four-year period. This tension and fear are factors that fuel "going postal," a dictionary distinction, and workplace violence.

While diversity initiatives include programs that will definitely help women, people of color and other minorities on the job, they will help Caucasian males as well. Some examples follow:

- More effective performance and career-planning initiatives to assist in identifying their development needs and in preparing them for promotional opportunities

- Benefits such as flexible schedules, child care, elder care and family leave that focus on males

- Managers trained to work with and respect diverse groups of people

These diversity initiatives help everyone by building employees' loyalty, reducing employee turnover and improving employee productivity.

A Spin-off of Gender: Sexual Harassment

Whatever the arguments — that it has always been around or that sexual tensions are normal — one fact is clear: Harassment is illegal, whether it focuses on sex, race or any other distinction. Sexual harassment is defined as deliberate or repeated behavior of a sexual or sex-based nature that is unwelcome, not asked for, or not returned by the person being harassed. The behavior could be verbal, nonverbal or physical. It's important to note that harassment is defined by the victim, and it is impact, not intent, that so labels it. A few examples follow:

- Derogatory or vulgar comments about someone's gender, physical anatomy or characteristics

- Sexually suggestive or vulgar language or jokes

- Threats of physical harm

- Sexually oriented or suggestive pictures, posters, magazines or other materials

- Touching someone in a sexually suggestive way or in a way intended to invade that person's personal space

- Touching or "accidentally" brushing against someone's breasts, genital area or derriere

On November 10, 1980, the EEOC issued a set of guidelines making sexual harassment a form of illegal sex discrimination. Those seven guidelines are summarized here.

1. Section A: Sexual harassment consists of unwelcome sexual advances, requests for sexual favors, and other verbal or physical conduct of a sexual nature. This type of behavior is illegal

    - When it is part of a manager's or supervisor's decision to hire or fire someone

    - When it is used to make other employment decisions about pay, promotions or job assignments

- When it interferes with an employee's performance

- When it creates an intimidating, hostile or offensive work environment

2. Section B: When deciding sexual-harassment cases, the EEOC will look at all circumstances on a case-by-case basis.

3. Section C: A supervisor is responsible for harassment by her employee whether or not the supervisor knows about the actions and whether or not the supervisor approves or disapproves of the behavior.

4. Section D: Employers are responsible for harassment of an employee if they know about it or know what actions should be taken to stop it.

5. Section E: An employer may be responsible if an employee is harassed on the job by people other than coworkers as long as the employer knows about the situation and fails to take appropriate action.

6. Section F: Employers should take all the necessary steps to prevent sexual harassment from occurring in the first place.

7. Section G: If an employee submits to sexual requests and professionally benefits from that, then the employer may be sued for sex discrimination by other employees who were equally qualified and denied those same benefits.

The EEOC reports that claims of sexual harassment are on the increase. In 1990, the EEOC recorded 6,883 complaints compared to nearly 16,000 in 1997 — an increase of about 150 percent in just seven years! Furthermore, the EEOC reports that the number of sexual-harassment cases settled rose from 7,484 in 1992 to 17,115 in 1998 and topped 20,000 by 2000.

The Center for Creative Leadership found that 90 percent of all women polled in a 2000 query think sexual harassment is a problem in the workplace. Furthermore, 70 percent of the women responding reported that they've been harassed at one time or another. However, less than 10 percent of victims ever file a formal complaint. And of those who do, the EEOC estimates that nine out of 10 victims settle out of court rather than face the embarrassment of confronting their harasser. Female victims are also nine times more likely than male victims to quit their jobs. Another indicator of gender differences is the fact that 67 percent of men say they would be flattered if propositioned on the job, while only 17 percent of women admit to the same feelings.

Some issues to consider when dealing with sexual harassment include:

1. What is the tolerance level for sexual harassment in the organization? While the answer must be zero, the issue is what is not considered harassment. This must be clearly addressed.

2. What is a "reasonable person" standard? This must be applied to determine if conduct is sexual in nature and to eliminate stereotypical notions of acceptable behavior. This considers the circumstances and environment.

3. In determining whether a behavior is unwelcome, it must be clear that there is no legal requirement or responsibility for the victim to warn or alert a harasser that a behavior is unwelcome.

4. Even though a person believes that sexual jokes are okay and a group is just having fun, she cannot make the joke-telling okay based on her own stereotypical notions.

5. Tangible employment action — misusing power or influence to make submission of sexual conduct a condition of employment or employment decisions — includes hiring; promotion; failing to promote; demotion; significant change in duties, compensation or pay decisions; and work assignment or reassignment.

6. Office romance, though not constituting sexual harassment when a consensual relationship, is not proper behavior in the workplace, suggests favoritism and violates the merit principles.

Nontraditional Lifestyles

Harassment threatens other groups in the workplace besides women.

Certainly men are sexually harassed and equally protected under the law. So are gays and transgendered workers.

People of nontraditional sexual orientation are a less-talked-about minority. With society's more open views, many feel less of a need to hide one's orientation; the prejudice, discrimination and negative preconceptions, however, still abound. People still judge a person based on their own religious or superstitious views, condemning a lifestyle that they erroneously believe is one of choice and not genetics.

Gays reflect the diversity of the population as a whole, representing all cultural, religious, ethnic, economic, social and age categories. Often they are designated the invisible minority; there is nothing that really sets them apart and they often choose to hide their sexual orientation, fearing the reaction of others.

Stereotypes abound and are often supported inadvertently in the workplace. If a man mentions his wife, his role as a spouse and not as a sexual partner is assumed; yet if a gay person mentions her personal life, she is perceived as discussing her "sex life."

Those who choose to reveal their sexual orientation may feel a sense of relief or an increased sense of self. Increased awareness of the number of people with a different sexual orientation as well as greater education on lifestyle differences allow gains to be made. In 1973, the American Psychological Association concluded that homosexuality, like any orientation, is not a disease, illness or deviance. Sexual orientation, which determines to whom someone is physically and emotionally attracted; whether gay, lesbian, bisexual or straight, is determined by genetics. Orientation does not equal behavior or choice. Understanding these distinctions will minimize homophobia, a fear or dislike of gays and lesbians.

Gay Rights

In addition to the laws protecting people from discrimination, groups have banned together to support diversity. The first national gay persons' group, the Mattachine Society, was formed in 1951. In 1969, an event known as Stonewall, named after the Greenwich Village gay bar and the riots that occurred after a police raid, launched the modern gay political movement and sparked the formation of the Gay and Lesbian Activists Alliance, the Gay Liberation Front and the Gay Academic Union. While some positions, like those of liberationists, are seen as extreme, many reformers promote this issue as a subculture with special needs and one that deserves recognition. Since 1997, the AFL-CIO has officially supported Pride at Work, a labor group that campaigns for acceptance and equality in the workplace. While anti-discrimination protection exists, only a few states prohibit firing workers because of sexual orientation.

Guarding Against Discrimination

Regardless of fear, prejudice and misinformation, a majority of Americans disapprove of discrimination and favor equal treatment in the workplace. One form of discrimination that is the equivalent of the "glass ceiling" is the "lavender ceiling." Some tips to foster diversity around this situation follow:

- Respect the privacy of all employees and especially the privacy of gay employees.

- Create a corporate culture in which gay employees are welcomed, accepted and valued for their contributions to the company. Include the issue of sexual identity in the company's diversity training programs.

- Break through the "lavender ceiling" by giving gay employees opportunities for advancement beyond low-level and mid-level management positions.

- Check company policies and union contracts for nondiscriminatory language regarding sexual orientation.

- Assist in the establishment of gay employee support groups and networks. Levi-Strauss and Disney offer examples.

- Check company policies and union contracts for benefits coverage for domestic partners. In 1991, Lotus, a software company, became the first major publicly held company to change its benefits policy to include all workers equally.

- Invite the domestic partners of gay and lesbian employees to company functions and make them feel welcome.

- Don't allow jokes about homosexuality to be told in the workplace. Establish a company policy for dealing with those who ignore warnings about discriminatory behavior.

- Make sure employees understand that HIV and AIDS are not just "gay" diseases and that HIV and AIDS can't be spread through normal workplace contact.

How to Handle Harassment

The best way to deal with any harassment is to stop it as soon as it starts. Don't let a situation get out of hand and become a matter for the courts. Victims of sexual harassment need to be assertive when responding to unwelcome advances or inappropriate material or jokes.

One way to respond is the "sandwich" method, which defines the offensive behavior at the top, explains why it's offensive in the middle, and then requests for it to stop at the bottom. Essentially the message takes on the characteristics of a sandwich. Here's an example of how it works.

When you ... massage my shoulder, squeeze my arm, touch my hand, make jokes about my relationships ...

I am … embarrassed, uncomfortable, angry …

Because … this is inappropriate, not right …

Therefore … I want you to stop.

After taking this initial action, a victim of harassment should consider telling her supervisor or reporting it to human resources. She also should seek out help from a support group, a trusted friend or counselor. Keeping a record is helpful. If another incident occurs, then the victim should definitely report it to her supervisor and the human resources department. They, in turn, should take appropriate action to stop the sexual harassment. A formal complaint should only be filed as a last resort.

If one of your associates informs you that she is a victim of sexual, verbal or physical harassment, take the charge seriously. Tell the employee you'll investigate the charge, then document and date all of your conversations. Maintain confidentiality, but do inform your company's human resources department about the charge. Be sure to remain objective when discussing the incident and get each person's side of the story, including those of any other people who witnessed it.

Questions to ask during an investigation follow:

- Who is the alleged harasser?

- What did she do specifically?

- Where did the incident take place?

- How did you respond?

- What were your feelings at the time? What are they now?

- Did anyone else witness the incident?

- Did you talk to anyone else about the incident?

- Is this the only incident or have there been others?

- Did you document the incident or incidents?

- What suggestions do you have for remedying the situation?

As a manager, take the following steps to prevent harassment:

- Express strong disapproval of sexual harassment.

- Make sure the company has a written policy about sexual, verbal and physical harassment. It should mirror the EEOC guidelines.

- Distribute the policy and discuss it with all employees. Give them specific examples.

- Inform employees of their rights and how to respond to harassment. Let them know that inappropriate incidents must be reported.

- Require employees to take training that covers sexual-harassment issues.

- Develop and carry out appropriate reprimands for employees who are found guilty of sexual harassment. Depending on the severity of the complaint, these may include termination, suspension, demotion or transfer.

Companies must take the issues of gender discrimination and all forms of harassment seriously. Those that don't open themselves up for potential lawsuits as well as morale problems among employees.

How do you handle gender issues? Answering the following questions will help you make an evaluation.

- Do you think pay and promotions are handled fairly?

- How is your organization made up in terms of women, gays and transgendered individuals?

- What accommodations do you feel are necessary for the special needs of women and gay people?

- Have you witnessed or experienced sexual harassment? How did you deal with it?

Would you consider any of the following as sexual harassment?

- A male supervisor has a tendency to look female employees up and down while talking with them.

- A female employee wears tight, short skirts to work, prompting some of her male coworkers to make sexual comments and jokes about her.

- A male employee hangs a picture of a woman in a bikini in his cubicle. This offends some of his female coworkers.

- Do you have an image of what a gay man looks like or how he acts?

- Do you have an image of a lesbian and how she acts?

Reflections

It's our responsibility to help rid the workplace of gender and anti-gay discrimination and prejudice. We can do this by challenging our own beliefs, biases and assumptions. We can also do it through educating ourselves.

Chapter 6 Summary

The workplace is no longer a white-male bastion with traditional gender roles and biases in evidence. Females continue to enter and reenter the workforce in large numbers. They bring skills and talents that complement the traditional "male" approach. Teamwork, communication and sensitivity are added. This is not to say that these aptitudes are not present in men; it is accurate to note that the increased gender mix allows a more versatile approach to relationships, communication and managing to be appreciated. As with the male-female issue, gays and transgendered people are misunderstood and unfairly treated, and their talents are not used to their full potential.

With these demographic changes, continued discrimination and common misperceptions come the need for more active management and greater education. Workplace discrimination often forces people to hide their true identities and stifle creativity and innate talents. Title VII of the amended 1964 Civil Rights Act says that men and women must be treated equally on the job, especially when it comes to hiring, firing, pay, promotions and benefits. Pay as well as promotions must be addressed. Strive for diversity among job applicants. Actions to take include the following:

- Offer competitive wages for jobs for both men and women.

- Develop a system for valuing the skills and responsibilities for each position in an organization.

- Refuse to allow harassment of any kind in the workplace.

- Offer training and counseling specific to gender issues.

- Recruit, hire and promote based on skill, talent and aptitude.

Realize and help your associates understand that diversity initiatives definitely help all people within the organization while strengthening the organization itself. What has been labeled "traditional" can no longer be argued — the 2000 Census shows us that there is no "traditional" anymore, not in family composition, not in individual preferences, not in staffing.

7 PERSONS WITH DISABILITIES AND THE PHYSICALLY DIFFERENT

Disability is a valid diversifier in the workplace. Consider who is disabled — someone you know, have worked with, have heard about. Consider those who have had an impact on you — Beethoven, perhaps, or Einstein, Janet Reno, Michael J. Fox, Ronald Reagan, Christopher Reeve, Stevie Wonder, Muhammad Ali, a relative or friend. An estimated 54 million Americans, over 20 percent of our population, have been identified as having one or more disabilities. This makes them the largest minority in America. Approximately one out of 11 will experience a significant, life-enduring disability, and nine out of 10 will experience a short-term disability (broken limb, surgery, hearing, visual loss).

Disabilities Defined

The term "persons with disabilities" is preferred when talking about individuals because it focuses on them first as persons. As a whole group of people, disabled is acceptable. Here are the preferred terms to use when describing a specific type of disability.

- Sight-impaired, visually impaired or blind

- Hearing-impaired or deaf

- Mobility-impaired

- Emotionally impaired

- Mentally impaired

- Neurologically impaired

There are two general types of disabilities: visible and invisible. Persons with disabilities are classified by

- Having a physical or mental impairment that substantially limits one or more major routine activities, such as seeing, hearing or walking

- Having a record of a physical or mental impairment

- Being regarded as having a physical or mental impairment

People are born with disabilities as a result of genetics, alcohol/drug abuse, poor prenatal care and birth trauma. Disabilities in later life are a result of accident, age, disease and illness. In other words, anyone can acquire a disability at any time regardless of race, gender, education, socioeconomic or any other status. Those with disabilities are at virtually every level in every career field. The vast majority of disabled persons want to lead lives that are as normal as possible as productive, valuable employees.

Managers certainly seem to view them that way. According to two Harris Polls conducted in the last decade, 80 percent of responding managers indicated that disabled employees were just as easy to supervise as employees without disabilities. Furthermore, half of these same managers gave their disabled employees higher marks for attendance, punctuality, reliability and work ethic. A review of 90 studies of disabled employees reveals that they actually have better safety records and equal or better turnover rates, absentee rates and job assignment flexibility.

Americans With Disabilities Act

During the 1960s, disabled persons began to band together to win recognition as a minority group entitled to certain rights and protection for those rights. In 1973, a federal law required federally funded organizations to end discrimination against disabled persons and to make their public facilities accessible to the disabled. This law didn't apply to most private companies or public places such as stores, restaurants and theaters.

In 1990, the Americans With Disabilities Act (ADA) was passed, becoming fully effective in 1994. The ADA is enforced by the EEOC, protects disabled persons from job discrimination in both government and private business, and guarantees them accessibility to virtually every facility open to the public. It has five major sections or titles.

1. Title I prohibits employment discrimination.

2. Title II requires state and local governments to provide accessibility and to prohibit employment discrimination (similar to the 1973 federal law).

3. Title III requires accessibility to stores, restaurants, theaters and all public facilities.

4. Title IV requires telecommunication accommodations, such as telephone-relay devices for the hearing-impaired.

5. Title V includes a variety of technical requirements.

To ensure that these requirements are met, most large companies have established employee task forces involving human resources and legal professionals. Small businesses have often turned to industry associations, chambers of commerce, consultants and attorneys to help them conform to ADA guidelines. Because ADA is a civil-rights law designed to deal with inequality, it mainly pertains to preemployment activities.

ADA and Hiring Guidelines

Job descriptions are very important, according to the ADA. They must be accurate, contain only essential job functions, and specifically state what tasks the job requires. For example, a job description stipulates that a printing press operator must lift 50-pound boxes of paper up to 30 times a day. If a disabled person can meet the job requirement, then the ADA says that person should receive equal consideration for the position.

When it comes to the actual interviewing and hiring process, ADA requires companies to make "reasonable accommodations" for disabled persons. What determines if an accommodation is "reasonable"? It's "reasonable" as long as it doesn't impose undue hardship on the employer. This determination is made on a case-by-case basis. The law requires that people with disabilities may apply for a job and obtain an application form, and have easy access to parking and the building. These accommodations remove barriers that make it difficult for a person to secure or perform work. Other examples of "reasonable accommodations" include:

- Employment tests. For example, if a job applicant is visually impaired, then an employer must read the contents of an employment test to him or provide the test in large type or in Braille.

- Job interviews. Interviewers cannot legally inquire about a job applicant's medical history or any mental or physical impairment. After a conditional job offer has been made, however, applicants are asked what kind of accommodations they need.

- Medical tests. These are not permitted until after an employee has been hired. And they have to be administered to all employees, not just disabled employees.

- Meetings and training sessions. These must accommodate the needs of all participants, allowing them to fully take part. Make sure physically disabled employees have easy access to the meeting room itself through ramps or elevators, as well as restrooms, drinking fountains, vending machines and even light switches. Sign-language interpreters for participants with hearing impairments and front seating plus large-print handouts for those with visual impairments may need to be arranged. These requirements relate to both the employer and the provider of training.

Avoid poor accommodations and the potential for embarrassment and lawsuits by sending out a "Special Accommodations Request" along with the meeting announcement and agenda. The request should ask participants to identify specific needs such as

- Special meeting or hotel accommodations for physical disabilities

- Special visual or audio equipment for visual or hearing impairments

- Sign-language interpreters

- Special food requirements because of diet (vegetarian, kosher, etc.) and allergies, diabetes and other health-related issues

- Any other special needs

Technological Advances

Technology has greatly leveled the playing field. In some cases, computer technology allows employees to work from their homes, reducing or even eliminating the need to commute to and from the job, which often poses challenges for the disabled. Technological devices can be adapted or individually programmed to meet a specific person's needs. Motorized wheelchairs and electronic lifts on vehicles make getting around and even driving much easier for those who have mobility impairments. The visually impaired can take advantage of several devices, including audiotapes, special computers, and printers that produce Braille documents from regular computer disks. These advances reduce a company's costs in providing support people and assistance.

For the hearing-impaired, there are hearing aids and other devices that amplify speaking voices and filter out background noises. In some cases, real-time caption writers — people who function much like court reporters — transcribe communications for those who are deaf or hearing-impaired. These are examples of technology available to help employees do their jobs.

Welcoming Persons With Disabilities Into the Workplace

There are several things to do to make people with disabilities feel welcome in the workplace.

- Show that top management supports the hiring and promotion of disabled employees within the company.

- Offer disabled employees the same kinds of training and advancement opportunities given to others.

- Require all employees to attend diversity training that focuses on working with disabled people. Use it to eliminate stereotypes and assumptions of ability.

- Realize that all disabled people aren't alike and shouldn't be treated alike. Each is a unique person with individual needs.

- Focus on what disabled employees can do, rather than on what they can't do.

- Explore opportunities for people with mental impairments to work for your company. For instance, sheltered workshops can provide highly committed and enthusiastic workers with contract jobs, such as simple assembly and packaging. The workers are typically trained and supervised by professionals who have experience with the mentally disabled.

Physical Appearance and Diversity

While physical appearance is not within the definition and does not fall under ADA, it can be disabling to the individual and can deprive an organization of talent and performance. Like it or not, appearance on the job makes a difference. Diversity issues included in this discussion are height, weight, complexion, dress, and socioeconomic status. In some instances, people are disfigured or simply not graced with what our society, culture and the news media have deemed "attractive."

A myth long believed in business is that people who are good-looking, tall and well-proportioned typically get the jobs, the raises, the promotions and the most sales. There have been arguments that attractive people tend to earn about 5 percent more than average-looking people, who tend to earn about 7 percent more than those less endowed. Furthermore, attractive people are perceived as more intelligent, honest, confident and friendly than others. When translated into actions, these beliefs are discriminatory and rob the workplace of talent and productivity.

Obesity

About one half of Americans are considered medically overweight, and as many as two million Americans are categorized as "morbidly obese." This means they weigh twice as much as the top of the medically recommended weight range for people of their height, build and age. Being medically overweight is defined as 25 extra pounds for an average 5'4" woman and 30 extra pounds for an average 5'10" man.

Discrimination against obese persons is a very real problem in our society, especially for women, and obesity is often looked at as a disability. Just being 20 percent overweight can result in fewer career opportunities and lower wages. Image consultants counsel that businessmen give up $1,000 in salary for every pound they're overweight. Among women, only 13 percent who earn more than $50,000 annually are obese, while 30 percent who are in the lowest income categories are considered obese.

A study of exit interviews in 2000 done by SHRM (Society of Human Resource Management) indicated that 90 percent of workers listed "acceptable weight" as important to a successful career and ranked it fourth behind intelligence, job qualifications and education. As one obese person put it, "We're the last safe prejudice."

Support groups and organizations banning discrimination against the obese have increased as television and films challenge the biases. One of these is the National Association to Advance Fat Acceptance (NAAFA), based in Sacramento, Calif. The support group's goals include the following:

- Getting employers to treat weight as a diversity issue

- Ensuring the civil rights of the obese

- Ensuring equal access to employment for the obese

- Changing people's perceptions of the obese through education, legislation and the courts

- Improving the self-esteem of obese people

Only recently have the obese gained some protection from employment discrimination. For instance, since the mid-1990s, some state courts have ruled that the morbidly obese are covered under the Americans With Disabilities Act. Claims of discrimination under the ADA must first be filed with the EEOC. Although the EEOC doesn't consider obesity a "traditional" disability, it has stated that looks shouldn't affect a person's ability to get and keep a job.

There's also protection for the morbidly obese stemming from the constitutional right to privacy. Specifically, it means that companies can't judge a person based on personal eating habits or lack of exercise. This position is backed by the American Civil Liberties Union.

Misconceptions About Appearance

As with all diversity qualifications, myths perpetuate stereotypes that in turn result in discrimination. Perceptions are unfounded on an individual level — whether they suggest disposition, attitude, productivity or talent. And, like any assumption, there is often a basis from which exaggeration occurs. For example, some physical characteristics strain health or tax one's ability to perform strenuous activities. However, this should not be an automatic disqualifier when applying for positions. If a job involves lifting 30-pound boxes, then let all applicants prove their ability to do the task.

If hired, some companies argue that their customers don't want to do business with people with certain appearances and that co-workers won't respect them. NAAFA and civil-rights groups counter by saying these are the same arguments used to resist equal rights for women and minorities for many years. If discrimination has been outlawed against these groups, then why not for the obese? Or the small people? Or the disfigured or tattooed?

Appearance and Success

The way people carry themselves, dress and fix their hair or make-up is completely within their control, as is hygiene. Culture can dictate personal preferences or habits; however, unlike disabilities, they can be readily addressed. In the workplace, there are formal or informal dress codes that employees are expected to follow. The new millennium favors a more casual attire, and it is increasingly poor form to judge a person by attire. In fact, ads — like the popular Microsoft ad that shows a group of people with pocket protectors and glasses with tape over the nosepiece, with the caption, "Would you have dated these people?" poke fun at such prejudice.

Help associates see these differences as signs of individualism. Things like hairstyle, body piercing and tattoos, clothing or shoe selection are certainly more acceptable now than ever before. Realize that they don't indicate or affect one's mental abilities or talents. They may, in fact, enrich creativity and suggest alternative thinking and decision making.

Handling Appearance Differences

Using customer surveys and performance reviews, study if appearance has an impact on productivity. If the facts support concerns, address them on specific behavioral levels. It's a good idea to establish written policies and procedures outlawing this type of discrimination. Some considerations to keep in mind include the following:

- People's ability to do their jobs. If someone is too short to operate a piece of manufacturing equipment, the solution is simple and straightforward. Give that person a special stool to stand on. Some issues, however, are more complex and less straightforward. Say a store clerk's job requires lifting boxes that weigh up to 30 pounds and climbing a ladder to stock shelves. In that case, the job probably wouldn't be appropriate for a morbidly obese person.

- Fair and equal pay. If a person can do the job, then he should be paid the same amount as other employees.

- Protection from hiring discrimination. Be objective in determining if a person can do the job, regardless of appearance.

- Protection from harassment. Don't allow other employees to malign and mistreat a person based on appearance. Include information about discrimination against obese persons and people with different physical appearances in a diversity training program.

- Special accommodations. Remember that because of their size or physical stature, employees may require special accommodations. For instance, they may need different office chairs in order to be comfortable. When traveling on business, they may need accommodations in cars and airplanes.

- Respect for privacy. Don't ask employees personal questions about their weight, eating habits, shopping, etc., that will embarrass them.

- Acceptance. Learn to accept people as they are. Appreciate them for their positive attributes and their contributions to the company.

- Effect on customers and income. In some cases, a company's sales and service may suffer if customers don't like the way an employee dresses, looks or acts. The best course of action is to find a compromise. If a waiter at a restaurant has pierced body parts that offend some customers, ask him to remove his body jewelry while working.

- Cultural, ethnic and religious expressions. Whenever possible, workers should be allowed to practice their customs or wear items that reflect their cultural, ethnic and religious backgrounds, as long as they do not interfere with the needs or the conduct of business.

- Safety issues. Again, look for compromises whenever possible. See if there's a hard hat made to accommodate the turban. Allow those working on a manufacturing line to wear dreadlocks as long as their hair is pulled back or secured by a hairnet.

- Training, education and reason can overcome beauty-standard prejudice and allow diversity to enrich the workplace. To make people feel welcome in the workplace, follow these guidelines:

  — Show that top management supports the hiring and promotion of diverse individuals.

  — Offer disabled employees and those who are weight-, height- or appearance-challenged the same kinds of training and advancement opportunities given to others.

  — Realize that regardless of appearance or categories, people aren't alike and shouldn't be treated alike.

  — Explore opportunities for people with mental or physical challenges to work for your company.

Imagine what it would be like to be visually impaired, hearing-impaired or mobility-impaired for just one day. How would you do your daily activities?

Go through the following list of activities and think about how each would be affected by a specific impairment.

	Visually Impaired	Hearing-Impaired	Mobility-Impaired
• Waking up and getting ready for work			
• Commuting to work			
• Completing tasks associated with your job			
• Communicating with coworkers, customers, etc.			
• Attending meetings			
• Eating lunch			
• Using the restroom			

How might each of the following jobs be "reasonably accommodated" to fit someone with a mental or physical disability, or a different appearance?

- An accountant

- A worker on a manufacturing line

- A secretary

- A manager of a large customer sales and service center

- A computer company CEO

- A maintenance worker

Reflections

Identify a coworker who looks very different from you and then answer the following questions:

Coworker _____

- What impression did you have of this person right after meeting him?
- At that time, how would you have described this person?
- Now that you know this person better, what is your impression of him?
- How would you describe this person today?
- How have your impressions changed over time?

Answer the following questions about your workplace:

- Does your company have a written or unwritten dress code?
- Briefly describe the dress code.
- How do you prefer to dress?
- Are there people in your workplace who have physical appearances that don't fit a social norm?
- How do people react to these different appearances?
- Is weight discrimination a factor in your workplace?
- How is nonconformity handled?
- Is there uniformity in appearance at the different levels within your organization?
- What does your employee handbook say about people with disabilities?
- What does your employee handbook say about people with weight concerns?
- What does your employee handbook say about people with extreme height differences?
- How do you fit into the norm in terms of mental or physical aptitude or appearance?

Reflections

Chapter 7 Summary

Employees with disabilities want to be seen as normal human beings, not as victims. They want to be treated with dignity and respect and given the same opportunities as their coworkers. Forward-thinking companies that do this receive much in return: loyal, dependable and productive employees.

The term "persons with disabilities" is preferred when talking about individuals who are sight-, hearing- or mobility-impaired; are emotionally, mentally or neurologically impaired; or who have learning disabilities.

Laws such as the Americans With Disabilities Act require fair and equal treatment for persons with disabilities while not placing undue hardship on an organization. There are more and inexpensive technologies that help a company gain a competitive advantage by employing a person with a disability. This goes for people with different-from-the-norm types of appearance characteristics. These include those not in one's control such as height or physical looks, as well as weight, dress, hygiene and body adornment.

Begin shifting your frame of reference and that of your associates, from "disability" awareness to "ability" awareness. Become more confident of individuals' skills in interacting comfortably with people whose appearances are different from our own.

After ADA was passed, from 1994 through 1996, more than 800,000 adults with "severe" disabilities entered the workforce. The talent shortages and growing need for specialized skills make all workers invaluable if they bring skill and aptitude into the workplace. Going beyond differences gives organizations the talent base they require.

8 DEVELOPING THE SKILLS REQUIRED FOR DIVERSITY TO WORK

While a diversity initiative includes knowledge and awareness of the variety of elements that characterize it, the positive impact of diversity is magnified if it goes beyond legal compliance and strengthens the skills that build awareness. Add to this a confronting of attitudinal barriers and diversity becomes more than a word used to recruit talented people.

Skills to make diversity work are more than politeness and etiquette. They go beyond teaching reason and judgment. They are, however, basic communication and interpersonal skills and they add to the innovation and stronger decision making that diversity yields. These include the following:

- Leadership
- Communication
- Management accountability
- Understanding of ROI
- Value awareness
- Open attitudes
- Recognition and reward
- Knowledge of people and culture

Because workers bring all sorts of backgrounds to the workplace, learning to understand and respect different behaviors and tendencies relies on skill training. The father of organizational development, Thomas Gilbert, taught to start with the outside, easy stuff and work into the hard, internal issues. Begin with behavior and end with attitude in order to foster diversity.

Where to Start Skill Development

Begin with awareness. Starting during the recruitment process tells potential employees that diversity is desired. Share the organization's diversity policy with potential and active employees. Let everyone know what is not tolerated. Clearly demonstrate the benefits to everyone. Build skills on knowledge, then move easily to strengthening interpersonal skills, communication skills and motivational skills.

Demonstrate how and why employees must step outside their comfort zones to experience and benefit from diversity. This requires people to challenge assumptions, to look within themselves to see the thinking ruts that deter reasoning. By insisting on polite and respectful communication, sensitivity is taught.

Good communication, for example, is the key to any business deal, but it's essential in dealing with diverse people. The first and most obvious barrier to communication is language. To deal with this, learn behaviors such as the following:

- Listen to what the other person is saying or attempting to say before interrupting or trying to help.

- Ask questions for clarification, not to put someone on the spot. For example, avoid a question like, "Why do you … ?" or "Why are you?" and use clarifiers such as, "How is it that … ?" "What does that mean?"

- Perfect your ability to give feedback. People of other cultures may have difficulty with the direct approach that characterizes American business.

- Minimize any frustration that others may have by seeking help from someone who could interpret.

- Observe body language and express empathy nonverbally by being attentive and nonthreatening.

Developing skills in listening, questioning and giving feedback will build understanding fast. Be careful with gestures, however, no matter how well intended. There is no universal body language. The common gesture of making a circle out of your thumb and pointer finger while holding your remaining three fingers straight means "okay" in the U.S. and United Kingdom and most of Europe. But if you use this gesture in France, it means "this person is a zero." For the Japanese it can mean "Please give me change." In some Mediterranean countries, it's used as an accusation or obscene characterization about another person. The following example shows the importance of clarifying meaning. A buyer of shirts representing a large department store chain from the Northeast was finalizing a large shipment from the factory of a Singapore immigrant. When asked if she would accept the offered $2.75 target price, the immigrant smilingly flashed the Asian sign for three, indicating her final offer was $3. The buyer thought he had scored with his low bid and was shocked when the shipment arrived far off budget.

Overcoming such misunderstandings involves the same skills as for connecting with others. They include:

1. Observation to develop awareness

2. Research through questioning and seeking information

3. Sensitivity to determine proper application

Understand Others' Languages

Developing skill in interpreting will minimize embarrassment and will further relationships. Here are a few prime examples why this is so.

*   When Coors translated its slogan, "Turn it loose," into Spanish, it became, "Suffer from diarrhea."

*   Pepsi's slogan, "Come alive with the Pepsi generation," became "Pepsi brings your ancestors back from the grave" in Chinese.

*   The Chinese language also proved troublesome for Coca-Cola. Originally the company's name was pronounced "Ke-kou-ke-la," which means "Bite the wax tadpole" or "Female house stuffed with wax."

- When Clairol introduced its "Mist Stick" curling iron in Germany, the company discovered that "mist" is a slang word for "manure."

Help reduce communication barriers for others. Take the African student who traveled to the U.S. to earn his MBA. Although he studied English for years and spoke fluently, he had trouble understanding some American phrases like "Cool it," "Hold that thought" and "Get out of town." The point is, language can be a barrier even when a person thinks she knows what someone is saying. Phrases, terms, slang, dialects and a host of other language nuances must be mastered for exchanges of information.

The Skill of Speech and Word Choice

Awareness and sensitivity identify words that are demeaning, degrading and show a lack of respect. Often this insight is lost in environments where no thought has been given to how another would interpret a phrase or comment. Words are extremely powerful as bridges or dividers. "Them's fightin' words" is a phrase to remember. Think back to a time when you felt devalued, can you really think words don't hurt?

Words have both a contextual and an emotional meaning. The dictionary definitions aren't a problem, but skill is required to avoid the common meanings that can infer less than positive things. Consider the word "creep." The dictionary says it means "to move slowly." Was that your first thought? How about the word "jerk"? Did "to pull fast" come to mind or were you insulted?

Awareness and sensitivity let us know that many people will take a literal meaning. Good use of English gives people a reservoir of multiple words from which to choose to convey correct meaning.

Labeling

It is difficult to avoid labeling. There are common, cultural assumptions and biases that have been attached to different people. Labels perpetuate myths that certain attributes or responsibilities are reserved for particular groups. These include anything from "middle-aged," "overweight," "gray-haired," "in debt," "the Scots," "Southerner" to "that lawyer." Labels simply short-circuit thinking and lump people together, robbing them and an organization of individuality and uniqueness. An example is of the woman who was explaining how she had fought in a meeting for a program, countering each statement with proof, factual evidence, figures and precedents. One of her associates complimented her saying, "Honey, you think like a man." Equally demeaning are comments like "women's work," "I'm not a women's libber, but ... " and going on to talk about an injustice. Skill is required to base communication on pertinent qualities, not sex or race.

Avoiding and Restricting Stereotypes

It takes skill to avoid promoting stereotypes. Such ways of thinking and reacting have, in many instances, developed into modern folklore. These images are so powerful that having personal friends or knowledge of key figures who are members of these groups does not contradict or change these stereotypical images.

Stereotypes usually suggest that all or most members of a racial or ethnic or other group are the same. Stereotypes lead to assumptions that are insupportable and offensive. They cloud the fact that all attributes may be found in all groups and individuals. Such stereotypes have included "aloof," "arrogant," "industrious," "artistic," "clannish," "aggressive," "angry," "lazy," "hustling," "sly," "alcoholic" or "blue-collar." Logic tells us that not all members of a group could be any one of the above. These descriptions spell out stereotypes and foster errors that communicators can make. For example, an employee may be describing a counterpart as "hard worker" and "burns the midnight oil," unconsciously portraying an exception to the mental images of the person.

Bias is subtle. The more deeply it has been assimilated, the more difficult it is to uncover and sometimes the more deeply it impacts the recipient. One example is the use of qualifiers to reinforce racial and ethnic stereotypes: "Mary Garcia, who has a degree, will be joining our staff" or "An articulate black professor spoke at our meeting." The qualifiers are added information that suggest an exception to the rule and imply that others don't have the qualities.

Eliminate Insensitive Terms

While a word or phrase may not be personally offensive, it can be to others. Words or phrases that could demonstrate insensitivity include:

- "Culturally deprived" or "culturally disadvantaged"

These terms suggest a superiority of one culture over another: "The company's efforts to assist culturally disadvantaged youths." A better way to address this is, "The company's efforts to assist youths whose heritage is Spanish, African, Asian … ."

- "Nonwhite"

The term implies that white is the standard. Terms such as "nonblack" or "nongreen" do not exist: "The policy aims to ensure equal treatment of nonwhite personnel." A more skilled way: "The policy aims to ensure equal treatment of staff members who are American Indian, African-American, Asian."

- "Minority"

This word ignores the fact that people of color comprise the majority of the world's population. The term is inappropriate as demographics change.

"The company's program for minorities" is less correct than "The company's program for employees of Indian or Filipino heritage … ."

- "Militant" or "activist"

These labels reveal personal or societal bias. An African-American involved in a social protest is called a militant, which suggests violence, while a white counterpart is called an activist. We must learn skill to correctly describe what we value.

Sexist Language and Racist Language

Anytime there is conflict between male and female or black and white, there are charges of sexist approach or racism. Churches are making contributions to erasing language discrimination by changes in liturgy, prayers and theological writings. Skill in developing job titles and job descriptions also facilitates diversity. Likewise, rid language of subtle forms of discrimination, such as those seen in the omission of women in references that take in humanity at large: "manpower" versus "workforce," "man hours" instead of "total hours," "mankind" versus "people."

Presentation skills will help eliminate potentially offensive terms for at least half of any communicator's audience today. Skill improvements here include:

1. Using plural personal pronouns that recognize both sexes and avoid discrimination. These include "they" versus "he," "him" or "his."

2. Substituting neutral words for "man" or "woman" in job titles. "Group" or "team" is more acceptable than "male" or "female."

3. Using parallel language when referring to persons by sex. Females over the age of 18 are "women." "Ladies" is appropriate only when men are called "gentlemen." Skewed references support stereotypic attitudes. Consider "man and wife" versus "husband and wife."

4. Granting equal respect to both women and men, trivializing neither.

5. Treating women with respect by eliminating the use of patronizing language. Don't use sexual innuendoes, jabs or puns, and avoid portraying women as weak or helpless and men as strong or brave.

Sensitivity Toward Older Workers

Prejudice against older workers is supported by language. In the book, *The Joy of Sex*, Dr. Alex Comfort notes that "a chauvinist never becomes a woman, a racist never becomes a black … yet we continue with the attitude that the old are inferior." We may be prejudiced against ourselves! Patronizing stories about the foibles of old age definitely hurt us.

Skill in portraying ageism carefully will help diversity as a whole. The media increasingly show active older persons who travel, play and engage in sports and business. Avoid labeling and limiting people with words. Terms to eliminate include:

- Twilight years

- Senior citizens

- Elderly

- Cute, sweet, dear, little, senile

- Out of date

- Over the hill

Actions that support diversity move away from myths and focus on the individual.

1. Enhance the self-esteem and self-confidence of older persons by respecting their knowledge.

2. Help younger people overcome their dread and disrespect of old age by showing what it is really like minus the stereotypes.

3. Draw all age groups together to recognize one another's needs.

4. Resolve serious problems by bringing them out in the open.

Sensitivity Toward Persons With Disabilities

The same is true of the skills required for sensitivity toward those with disabilities.

- Be sensitive to abilities rather than disabilities.

- Recognize that "disability" and "handicap" do not mean the same thing. Disability means not able to do something; handicap indicates an inability to perform a task as well as a nonhandicapped individual.

- Develop a bias-free attitude toward disabilities.

- Avoid mentioning disability when it is not pertinent.

Move from valuing diversity to cultivating its benefits — innovation, creativity, problem solving, talent — by actively cultivating the skills that move beyond tolerance. Shifting beliefs and attitudes away from "You're just like me" to "We are so unique" becomes a competitive advantage and real business need.

When you consider ways to benefit from diversity, most people think in terms of eliminating discrimination or changing attitudes toward differences.

Where do you see areas of greatest concern in terms of diversity?

What are the skills you require to address those concerns?

How can language be a tool for any skill enhancement in dealing with diversity?

What are some words or phrases that perpetuate stereotypes and biases in your workplace?

What is one guideline for speaking with, of or about a person different from you?

Reflections

Chapter 8 Summary

In order to succeed, today's workplace requires different skills and expertise than the workplace of our grandparents. Reading, writing and arithmetic are important, as is English. But judgment, careful use of language, and sensitivity to others' points of view are critical.

Word usage can promote or minimize stereotyping, demeaning comments and expressions that belittle. Labeling is one form of word usage that is a subtle form of negative communication.

Skills focus on awareness, sensitivity and communication. They emphasize how to connect with others and form relationships of respect and trust. They move people from assumptions and thinking ruts to being able to express reason and logical thought when dealing with others. Improved listening allows people to pick up on what is a sensitive issue for another person. The ability to question, not interrogate, can provide knowledge of what to do, how to speak, and when and where to offer assistance.

Kindness and good intentions alone will not improve diversity. Actions that are conscious and competent will minimize and tear down discrimination and disrespect. What is a must, however, for dealing with diversity is personal responsibility. We must all develop skills.

The Reverend Martin Niemuller expresses the need for personal responsibility in his powerful statement: "In Germany, the Nazis first came for the Communists, and I didn't speak up because I wasn't a Communist. Then they came for the Jews, and I didn't speak up because I wasn't a Jew. Then they came for the trade unionists, and I didn't speak up because I wasn't a trade unionist. Then they came for Catholics, and I didn't speak up because I was a Protestant. Then they came for me, but by that time there was no one left to speak for me."

Whether we are in a majority or a minority, in a group or a member of a team, we are all people whose combined skills add much to our organization. And ourselves.

9 MANAGING DIVERSITY

Well-known corporations such as AT&T, Digital and PepsiCo offer diversity training and awareness classes for their employees. It's a good practice for all businesses — no matter what their size — and is seen as a first defense for discrimination claims. Microsoft spokespersons said it well when noting, "A diverse company is better able to sell to a diverse world." A study by the consulting firms of Towers Perrin and the Hudson Institute found that one-fourth of 645 companies answering their 1996 survey were training their managers to handle a diverse workforce. More than half of the companies responding also indicated concerns about their managers' abilities to motivate and work with a culturally diverse group of employees.

The best way to manage diversity is to include everyone, moving from a corporate position down to individual responsibility, from behavior to attitude. Build a climate that supports all types of employees. This can be done by commitment, by identifying and addressing management challenges and by training — both formal and informal. Start by studying who has succeeded.

Companies Who Are Succeeding Through Diversity

Time, *Fortune*, the *Financial Times* and many others in the business media designated GE as the best-managed company of the century. GE immediately responded to the honor by noting that what makes them most respected and what drives performance is their employees, people from all over the world with diverse ideas and experiences. Each strategy and business initiative pulls from shared learning and combined know-how.

Diversity at GE has been a continuous process of cultural change. GE capitalizes on its workforce diversity by a set of values that provides all employees with a shared vision. The "boundarylessness" that Jack Welch, manager of the century, describes is based on the requirement to have leaders with the capacity to "build diverse and global teams," and to have leaders with "self-confidence to involve everyone." Welch taught how to gain by diversity when he relentlessly gave management directive. "It means engaging every mind on every problem, leaving no one out, weighing no one's ideas heavier because of the color of their skin, their gender, their nationality or whatever."

Pitney Bowes has a culture that demonstrates the value of every employee and the ability to leverage that diversity into business results. Pitney Bowes attributes its success to diversity and the insistence on leaders promoting it. Its global agenda emphasizes strategic commitment to support minorities who bring imagination into problem solving, to leverage a unique and diverse workforce and to recognize and capitalize on the talent and productivity of its people. This, the leadership insists, is what will sustain their competitive leadership well into the 21st century.

"Fostering diversity and taking advantage of its many benefits is not only the right thing to do, but is critical to its future," states Chase leaders. The diversity efforts of all its businesses in every major location worldwide have formed employee-led diversity councils, giving employee-diversity champions a real opportunity to define issues and implement solutions. All employees, from senior managers to ground-level associates, attend training. Mentoring programs focusing on career mobility and many innovative employee-focused benefits make the company attractive to talent.

Learn From Success

According to SHRM (Society for Human Resource Management), 75 percent of Fortune 500 companies have diversity programs in place and over 58 percent have staff dedicated to diversity issues. The Center for Creative Leadership surveyed managers at more than 300 Fortune 1000 organizations, including 71 from the Fortune 500 Industrials and 24 from the Fortune 50. They identified the most prevalent initiatives to be policies against racism and sexism, active affirmative action/equal employment opportunity (AA/EEO) committees or offices, internal audits or employee attitude surveys, and company-sponsored access to external training and seminars.

These experts highlight seven strong actions for effective attitudinal change and corporate support:

1. **High-level support and a strong message.** In *Implementing Diversity*, Marilyn Loden assessed initiatives in leading-edge companies and found that the most successful programs began with a strong business directive linking diversity to goals. Add to that consistent and visible sponsorship from the highest levels, and diversity becomes a part of the corporate culture.

2. **Mentoring programs.** Involving employees of the same and different races and backgrounds helps minorities who in the past were left out of most mentoring, which focused on white managers mentoring white youth. Whether formal or informal, mentoring guarantees future skills.

3. **Expanded definition of diversity.** Putting policies in place to expand the definition of diversity to include disability, family structure and lifestyle breathes life into other programs and promotes parity. Such policies provide goals everyone can support, like job-sharing, child care, and partner benefits.

4. **Statistics to persuade.** Credible, relevant facts about the business objectives and outcomes support successful initiatives and best persuade others to change. Using guilt and right-thing-to-do speeches don't trigger compliance.

5. **Programs for identifying and developing top talent.** Don't rely on recruitment to get diverse employees into the talent pool. Invest early and consistently in development and retention.

6. **Management accountability.** Link diversity goals to performance evaluation, compensation, promotion and succession planning. When such rewards are directly linked to meeting diversity goals, then diversity takes hold throughout the organization. Hold people accountable.

7. **Education programs that offer awareness and practical help.**
   The most effective education programs are ongoing and focus on specific interpersonal skills to help employees with communication and conflict resolution. Develop training specific to your corporate culture.

Active Management Practices

Fast Company magazine states: "You have the most to learn from people who are least like you. People who are different from you give you a completely different perspective. It is hybrid thinking — a blend of your view and the alternatives — and is critical to managerial success."

To get managers and all employees to blend and work together better

- Be alert to changes, especially changes in relationships. Are employees' work relationships changing? Is there hostility among workers? If so, what or who is fueling the conflict? How well do workers relate to one another? What are the unique characteristics and backgrounds of the people working around you?

- Talk and listen to others to constantly raise your awareness level. Read up on diversity issues to keep well-informed. Communication and knowledge can help ward off potential problems.

- Share personal values and beliefs with others and find out about their values and beliefs. This process usually helps pinpoint and uncover personal biases and blind spots.

- Find ways to value uniqueness. All workers can contribute to a company's success. Sometimes it's a matter of finding the best way for them to make a contribution. The whole is greater than the sum of its parts.

Clashes and Communication

See disagreement as inevitable and instead of viewing these clashes as negative and destructive, encourage associates to see them as opportunities.

- Recognize what makes people unique.

- Turn differences into compromises.

To communicate more effectively, develop the following:

- A high degree of trust and confidence among everyone

- Mutual respect and cooperation among everyone

- Full participation by all

- Acceptance of differences among employees

- Shared leadership

- Decisions based on compromises and consensus

Managing in this way creates an environment in which all employees feel comfortable expressing themselves. Traditionally, employees have had to rely on their managers for direction, information and ideas, thus creating one-way communication. However, when communication is two-way between a manager and employees, satisfaction on the job increases and so does productivity, according to several studies.

Research like this suggests that employees who are satisfied and talk about it perform the best. Employees who are dissatisfied and don't talk about it perform the worst. Also, those who are satisfied but don't talk about it rank lower in overall performance than those who are dissatisfied but talk. So, employees who may not be fully satisfied, but who at least work in an environment where they feel free to discuss things, can outperform those who work in an environment that discourages open communication.

Manage Innovation and Outside-the-Box Thinking

Two lessons of diversity are practicing open communication and exploring new ideas. Keeping aloof defeats the goal of mutual growth and productivity. Members of a dominant culture should practice the following:

- Resist trying to change others. Accept them as they are.

- Examine traditions for unfair practices, then work to change them.

- Ask sensitive questions to learn about others.

- Recognize cultural diversity and expand narrow views.

- Recognize that when an employee is under pressure, he may revert to narrow points of view.

- Support, train, coach and mentor others to help them grow.

People who don't belong to a dominant culture should follow these guidelines:

- Share personal distinctive qualities with others.

- Resist interacting or socializing only with those from their own culture.

- Respect themselves, their culture and the other cultures they're exposed to.

- Learn about the dominant culture from those around them.

Strive for inclusiveness. Communication is the key to building rapport among employees. By being silent and avoiding issues, people aren't really being kind or sensitive.

Mentoring

Being mentored or serving as a mentor is one of the best ways to cultivate hybrid thinking. The mentoring process brings all kinds of diverse people together in a positive, learning situation. Mentoring typically crosses divides of age, but it can also cross gender, race, religious and cultural divides as well. It is an advantage to both recruitment and retention.

At Procter & Gamble, "reverse mentoring" is practiced. Seasoned senior executives are taught about issues facing younger female employees. One of the lessons learned: The term "work-family balance" doesn't address the needs of single people who also may have many commitments outside of work.

Some of the problems of past mentoring programs included lack of time, fear of the other taking one's job, and lack of value placed on the practice. The good old boy or women's support groups handled it. Now, however, with talent wars and growing competition, mentoring is a valued and, in many companies, a formal development program. Pieces to consider in initiating a mentoring program include:

- Forget about age and level within a company. Base choices on skill and potential.

- Match partners by assignment or by allowing either the mentor or the high-potential individual to choose.

- Allow the individuals to determine the time, frequency and place they will meet.

- Allow individuals to determine context and content of their meetings. Some benefit from simply talking; others like a formal on-the-job training relationship.

- Recognize and reward mentoring programs.

Training Programs

Whether conducted in-house or off-site, diversity training programs make employees more aware of the issues and needs of all of their coworkers. A good program results in three things:

1. Workforce unity rather than separatism

2. Comfort with, rather than ignorance about, diversity

3. A work environment where employees feel valued and respected

Everyone benefits from diversity training — from the stockholders and board to the president and CEO and to the teams and front-line associates. Training surveys have long shown that "attitudinal" training is most effective with upper management's full support. A consistent challenge is getting management "buy in." A Yankelovich Partners survey conducted in 1996 showed that while a majority of business CEOs saw the purpose and value of diversity training, most didn't want to deal with the potential problems associated with starting a program. Some suggestions for getting a diversity initiative off the ground with top management's support follow:

- Tailor diversity training to fit the company's culture and business. For example, someone who works for an accounting firm might use lots of statistics to back up his ideas. On the other hand, someone in the entertainment industry might try a series of skits depicting important diversity issues.

- Expand executives' views of diversity beyond race and gender issues. Explain how religion, education, family and socioeconomic background play a part in diversity, too.

- Make a strong business case for diversity training. Show how valuing people's differences can increase morale, productivity and profitability. If possible, use statistics and concrete examples.

- Be prepared and take advantage of the available time. Provide upper management with a well-thought-out diversity awareness and training plan. Ask for their commitment on the spot. Remind them that "do as I say, not as I do" won't cut it.

Still, some employees may hesitate to actively participate in diversity training discussions. They may fear asking the wrong questions, using the wrong terms, offending others or being misunderstood, or even going against their fellow workers' views. While these are valid concerns, they must not stand in the way of forging new and more positive relationships with their co-workers.

If diversity remains a nondiscussible topic to workers, who are allowed to "feud" or fall back on group norms, there will be only conflict and petty grievances. Work will be affected and morale low. Explain how diversity positively affects everyone. Diversity training can be successful simply by pounding it into people's heads that people are different and similar. Teach associates the following:

- How each person thinks. Be sure discussions involve the human thought process and how assumptions and stereotypes are formed.

- Emotional training. This should examine issues of personal prejudice and stereotyping in depth.

- Organizational cultural training. A company-wide approach to diversity training should explore how the corporate culture, reward system, training and promotional practices support or undermine the success of a diverse work environment.

While there are all kinds of diversity training and awareness initiatives, some of the most common topics are as follows:

- Diversity: Blending a Multicultural Workforce

- Nondiscrimination in the Workplace

- Sexual Harassment in the Workplace

- Americans With Disabilities Act (ADA) and Hiring

- Employment Law Awareness

- New Action in Affirmative Action

To cover all the complexities of diversity training, employees need to spend more than cursory "let's satisfy legal concerns" time in a session. To make real and lasting changes in attitudes and behaviors, organizations must first establish policies against discrimination and harassment. Then they must set up ways to monitor attitudes and behaviors as well as ways for employees to register complaints against co-workers who violate the policies.

Companies also can initiate activities that show all workers are valued. These activities include:

- Minority focus groups or support groups, where workers can openly discuss their special needs (Women of AT&T, National Society of Black Engineers)

- Quality councils, suggestion committees and open-communication forums that involve all employees

- Using appraisal and discipline techniques that are applied equally and without prejudice

- Establishing codes of conduct that clearly state how employees should communicate and behave on the job

- Making diversity awareness and training a requirement for promotions

Codes of Conduct

Most large companies already have a code of conduct, which is included in employee handbooks and fully explained during the hiring process. Because the federal government enforces affirmative-action programs and EEOC compliance, adherence to these are often listed in a company's code of conduct. However, it's a management imperative to go beyond these government regulations and to promote diversity as a positive step in the continued growth of the company.

Setting codes of conduct regarding diversity creates a neutral, comfortable work environment for everyone. For example, a company might establish a policy that says all written communication should include both genders. That means all company reports, memos, newsletters, news releases, fliers, etc., should reflect both the "he" and "she" pronouns when talking about employees. In addition, codes of conduct typically deal with issues of sexual harassment, ethics, promotional practices, discipline and employee dress.

If your company doesn't have a code of conduct, develop one. If there is one, update it regularly to reflect the ever-changing world. There are resources to help draft or strengthen a code of conduct. Start with other firms in the same industry, the local chamber of commerce, legal counsel, a human resources consultant, and the Internet or local library. A book to consider is *Executive's Handbook of Model Business Conduct Codes* by Walter W. Manley II (Prentice Hall, 1991). Using many sources with different viewpoints helps eliminate any sexist or culturally biased language.

In its final form, a code of conduct should do several things including:

- Improve your company's public and consumer image.

- Encourage positive worker behavior.

- Encourage open and honest communication.

- Enhance morale, loyalty and recruiting efforts.

- Act as a catalyst for constructive change.

- Help reduce the number of improper, illegal, immoral or unethical acts performed by a company's employees.

- Provide specific guidelines to help employees spread the company's vision, including its commitment to diversity.

Provide all employees with your company's code of conduct. To manage distribution, consider having employees sign and return a form indicating that they read and agree to the document. Finally, for the code of conduct to be truly effective, managers must live by it. When managers fail to "walk the talk," employees take notice and lose respect for them and the company.

Beyond Doing the Right Thing

When employees are exposed to both diversity training and awareness initiatives, they're more likely to change their attitudes and basic beliefs. Managing diversity results in higher productivity, better teamwork among employees, greater profitability, and increased competitiveness in an increasing global marketplace.

Managing diversity requires managing preconceived biases. In the following scenarios, identify the sweeping generalizations that one might make. Then identify a management action that you could take.

- Scenario One: You have a new coworker who is from a different culture than yours. He helps himself to some supplies from your desk without asking.

  Generalization:

  Possible preventative action:

- Scenario Two: A supervisor dresses very poorly and drives a beat-up old wreck to work. His memos often have grammatical mistakes. He started out on the manufacturing line and worked his way up to a supervisory position.

  Generalization:

  Possible preventative action:

Reflections

Reflections

- Scenario Three: You call the maintenance department about getting a light fixture replaced. Someone who doesn't speak English very well is sent to make the repair but doesn't understand your instructions.

  Generalization:

  Possible preventative action:

- Scenario Four: A manager doesn't want to be bothered by mentoring a new hotshot in the department. But rather than say no, he misses appointments and, when together, says little.

  Generalization:

  Possible preventative action:

- Scenario Five: Upper management has committed to supporting a diversity initiative. No senior members, however, have signed up for any of the meetings. When invited, they are consistent no-shows.

  Generalization:

  Possible preventative action:

Reflections

Reflections

Chapter 9 Summary

Realizing or endorsing diversity is one thing. To make it a reality, however, management must take action — on every level within a company. One way to determine what to anticipate and what to do is to learn from the many companies that have diversity initiatives and which attribute financial success, recruitment ease and retention benefits to them. These companies include GE, Pitney Bowes, Chase, Xerox, DaimlerChrysler, Crayola and Microsoft.

Leveraging America's diversity is a top business priority for these and multiple other organizations. There is no disputing the fact that organizational cultures modeled on homogeneity are out of step with today's dynamic market conditions.

Mergers and acquisitions, downsizing and retention demand press companies to work together. System flexibility is central to this drive for innovation and collaboration. Both research and experience have shown that well-managed, heterogeneous groups will generally outperform homogeneous ones in problem solving, creativity, and solution building, exactly the capabilities on which business success increasingly depends.

Management efforts to make company diversity even more pivotal to competitive advantage amidst the exponential changes occurring include:

- Active management practices

- Open and continuous communications

- Trust building

- Requiring respect and appreciation for differences

- Mentoring programs

- Training programs

- A code of conduct

The most successful way to manage diversity remains "walking the talk." MBWA (management by walking around) that Tom Peters favors, the golden rule believed by so many, Covey's *Seven Habits*, individual responsibility — all will work, but all require management to take action. Managing diversity begins like all other management journeys, one step at a time.

10 DIVERSITY'S MANY OPPORTUNITIES AND BENEFITS ·

The U.S. labor force is now more diverse than ever before — and that's a great thing, since globalization, multinational partnerships, foreign sourcing, total quality management, and shrinking talent bases are redefining the way business is done. Dramatic changes have occurred: Women, people of color, immigrants surging into the workforce, older workers, gay and lesbian workers, the disabled and single parents are shifting the complexion of corporate cultures.

Leveraging America's diversity is a top business priority as organizations discover that business models of homogeneity are out-of-step with today's dynamic market conditions. The fact is that diverse workers create better work teams and make better decisions. Studies done on self-directed work teams found that 65 percent of heterogeneous teams — those composed of diverse workers — produced "high-quality" decisions or solutions that provided new or exceptionally effective approaches to problems. By comparison, for homogeneous teams — those composed of similar workers — the percentage of "high-quality" decisions was only 21 percent. Other team studies have shown that when given a creative task, heterogeneous teams adopt multiple strategies and identify more solutions than their homogeneous counterparts.

The Competitive Advantage

Company diversity is an even more pivotal competitive advantage amidst the enormous market shifts throughout the world. Many changes present huge opportunities for foreign investment — no more USSR; the European free market; the linking of the U.S., Canada and Mexico as a trading unit; and China and the Pacific Basin seen as new economic players. All require sensitivity and knowledge of the regions and cultures in order to negotiate, persuade and mutually benefit.

In America, diversity provides a competitive advantage with regard to its customers. African-Americans, Hispanics and Asian-Americans have an estimated combined spending power of over $650 billion. The nexters have seemingly bottomless pockets for shopping sprees and Gen X'ers are showing themselves as savvy investors in the stock market as well as strong spenders in the entertainment and service areas. The shift to a service economy increases the value of diverse employees who may be better able to relate to and negotiate with customers.

Companies that hire and utilize diverse workers will prosper in today's competitive economic environment, while those staying with the status quo will be left behind. During the 1990s, the U.S. labor force grew only 10 percent, as compared to the '80s with an 18 percent increase and the '70s with a 30 percent increase. Competition for top talent is fierce in the first decade of the 21st century. Highly skilled workers demand a career track and look for others like them in the upper echelons, or they look elsewhere.

Costs of Noncommitment

If "carrots" such as increased productivity and global-marketing effectiveness aren't always enough to initiate change in valuing diversity, the concomitant "sticks" of turnover costs or discrimination litigation might be. It can cost $112,000 to recruit and train a full-time sales employee at $1,000,000 a year. And that doesn't account for lost accumulated company knowledge or low morale where turnover is high. To estimate costs of front-line workers, factor in recruitment costs — time spent in analyzing the job, drafting ads, advertising, screening, interviewing and testing, uniforms, orientation, on-the-job training and formal training. Don't forget the average two weeks to three months of nonproductivity as they are learning. For ease, figure three to five times their salary.

Legislation including the Family and Medical Leave Act (FMLA), Americans With Disabilities Act (ADA), Age Discrimination in Employment Act, Immigration Reform and Control Act, and others noted in Chapter 1 shows a national resolve about workforce diversity. EEOC complaints reflect the emphasis: Sex-related complaints have increased 3 percent over the last decade, and disability cases are up 21 percent since the passage of ADA. In court, discrimination judgments run to $1 million, plus the 10 percent – 15 percent legal fees and cost of lost management time. Millions more may be lost in negative publicity. Corporate image is expensive to build and costly to maintain.

Employees Are Assets

As the marketplace becomes more and more competitive, as the life cycles of our products and services get shorter, as customers become more demanding and litigation increases, employees are an organization's greatest assets. Empowering them increases those assets. Diversity is the means of empowering all employees at all levels. An organization's long-term effectiveness comes directly from its ability to strengthen its workers. Valuing diversity brings the following:

- Greater vision by seeing through many eyes

- Greater opportunity for worker involvement

- Greater productivity as people learn to blend and work collectively

- Greater customer satisfaction

Realizing the true value and full potential of each employee yields loyalty. Loyal employees take pride in their work, they're willing to go the extra mile when it's needed, and they usually stick around for a long time. Long-term employment pays off at a time when the two greatest challenges today are recruitment and retention.

The Business Drivers

Going back to the beginning of this handbook, workforce diversity has become a major management strategy simply because it makes good business sense. Corporate commitment creates and sustains the open, supportive, responsive organization that diversity facilitates. When differences are acknowledged and valued, multiple drivers realized are

- How business is conducted today

- Changing workforce demographics that require it

- Talent retention efforts that demand it

- Productivity that is improved by it

- Teamwork that is enhanced by it

- A global business world that is cross-cultural

- Legal and compliance issues that are real

Actions to Realize the Benefits

Proactively, several things can be done to personally establish diversity as a business imperative.

1. Educate managers and associates on how to formulate a position that balances individual opinions with the behavior encouraged by diversity.

2. Avoid assumptions about who others are and how they should behave.

3. Share everything learned with associates and encourage one another to adopt productive behaviors.

4. Use inclusive language in all communications.

5. Encourage coworkers to be part of the social groups formed at work, including bringing partners to functions when appropriate.

6. Take time to understand the local laws and ordinances that relate.

7. Demonstrate an awareness of inclusiveness whenever possible.

There are also reactive actions to personally take to achieve the above-mentioned opportunities.

1. If someone confronts you with an opinion about another person, be open, saying you don't know how to respond to assumptions.

2. Refuse to laugh at discriminatory "humor."

3. Cite company policy about nondiscrimination, or walk away from a group verbally ridiculing or discriminating against a person or class.

4. Encourage others to read, attend events, and learn about different points of view and cultural dictates.

5. Tell others that their discriminatory behavior, verbal or nonverbal, is unacceptable.

6. Report incidents of discrimination to human resources or appropriate persons.

Measuring Success

Bringing a diverse team together and making it work require both active and reactive behaviors by every individual. To see progress as well as to motivate, establish a measurement system. Some steps to do this include:

1. Set goals specific to the roles and responsibilities of the team members. For instance, managers might require everyone on their teams to attend a two-day diversity awareness and training seminar. Then every six months, managers might hold a mandatory team-

building activity, such as delivering used clothing and toys to a battered women's shelter or working a school breakfast program.

2. Clearly communicate the goals to everyone on the team. Put goals in writing and make them a part of each team member's personal goals and objectives for the year.

3. Continually evaluate the team's performance. If someone isn't meeting the desired goals, schedule a periodic performance review. Go over the specific improvements for that person to make.

4. Reward the team's successes. Have a lunch delivered to the office or plan a fun team-building activity, such as quitting work an hour early to go bowling.

Diversity Checklists

There's no "I" in the word "team." To build a strong work team, blend together the individual strengths of each team member.

- Accept the fact that when it comes to people, "different" is normal.

- Learn to value these differences.

- Develop a comfort level in dealing with diverse types.

- Eliminate stereotypical judgments.

- Create opportunities for all workers.

When companies successfully integrate diversity into the workplace, it results in a win-win situation for everyone. Valued workers return their worth tenfold because they have the power to reach their full potential. Just as important, managers can take pride in their employees. Managers know they've been successful when diversity naturally becomes part of their company's corporate culture. The results are higher creativity, productivity and employee involvement. The benefits are at every level — personal, interpersonal and organizational.

Think about your coworkers and associates.

- How many of them grew up in the same decade?

- How many grew up in the same country, state, city or neighborhood?

- How many attended the same schools?

- How many have the same hobbies or enjoy the same leisure-time activities?

- Is everyone aware of the policies regarding diversity, affirmative action and sexual harassment?

- Is everyone aware of the value and benefits of diversity?

- Are individual team members sensitive to diversity issues?

- Is your diversity policy consistently implemented?

- Are the same tolerance levels and discipline procedures used for all employees?

- Are people trained to adhere to these policies?

- Is there support from top management?

- Do you actively support your company's or organization's policies regarding diversity, in all its forms?

Reflections

Chapter 10 Summary

Diverse workers create better work teams and make better decisions. Moreover, employees are an organization's greatest assets. To make diversity work and to help the company reach its full potential, empower everyone to think of their individual differences as strengths.

- Be alert to changes, especially changes in relationships.

- Talk and listen to others to constantly raise awareness.

- Share personal values and beliefs with others and find out about their values and beliefs.

- Find ways to value uniqueness.

Company diversity is about more than the competitive advantages it brings and the better workplace it fosters, and even more than global expansion and customer demographics. It's about participating in change and a changing world, about being a real player in life. Diversity can mean achieving America's age-old business goal of doing good while doing well. It can mean succeeding in a new millennium by taking the high road and seeing a strong return on investment.

As Kahlil Gibran noted:

"Work is love made visible. And if you cannot work with love but only with distaste, it is better that you should leave your work and sit at the gate of the temple and take alms of those who work with joy."

INDEX

SIXTY-MINUTE TRAINING SERIES™ 60

HOW TO
COACH AN
EFFECTIVE TEAM
LEADERSHIP THAT GETS RESULTS

BY MICKI HOLLIDAY AND JOE GILLIAM

NATIONAL PRESS PUBLICATIONS
A Division of Rockhurst University

Successful leaders know that team members need consistent coaching, mentoring and counseling to develop their skills, motivate them and spark their interest and enthusiasm. In this concise, easy-to-follow handbook, you'll learn how to:

◆ Get rid of your "manager's mentality" — and start thinking more like a leader
◆ Identify your team's varying needs at each stage of its development — from infancy through maturity
◆ Treat your team members as individuals, and celebrate everyone's efforts and contributions
◆ Determine when your people will benefit most from coaching, counseling or mentoring tactics
◆ Encourage creative solutions, "outside the box" thinking and open discussion and idea-sharing
◆ Assess when it's best to cheer your team from the sidelines, and when active leadership is the answer

Item #4308

$14.95

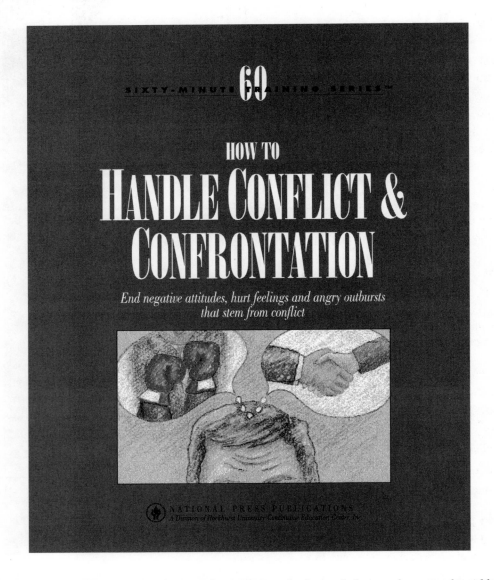

60
SIXTY-MINUTE TRAINING SERIES™

HOW TO
HANDLE CONFLICT & CONFRONTATION

End negative attitudes, hurt feelings and angry outbursts that stem from conflict

NATIONAL PRESS PUBLICATIONS
A Division of Rockhurst University Continuing Education Center, Inc.

Poorly handled conflicts cause anxiety, tension and stress in the workplace, reduce morale and hinder productivity. In this handbook, you'll discover a wealth of conflict management techniques for creating a more cohesive and What you will learn will help you:

◆ Understand why it's dangerous to ignore even the smallest conflict in hopes it will "just go away"

◆ Avoid four basic situations that will automatically trigger conflict between individuals

◆ Deal effectively with each of these conflict types: Substantive, Personalized and Communicative

Put the principles of How to Handle Conflict and Confrontation into action ... and start generating results and building a more creative and productive workplace today!

Item # 4952 $14.95

Buy any 3, get 1 FREE!

BUY 3 GET 1 FREE!
buy more, save more!

Get a 60-Minute Training Series™ Handbook FREE ($14.95 value)* when you buy any three. See back of order form for full selection of titles.

These are helpful how-to books for you, your employees and co-workers. Add to your library. Use for new-employee training, brown-bag seminars, promotion gifts and more. Choose from many popular titles on a variety of lifestyle, communication, productivity and leadership topics. Exclusively from National Press Publications.

DESKTOP HANDBOOK ORDER FORM

Ordering is easy:

1. Complete both sides of this Order Form, detach, and mail, fax or phone your order to:

    Mail: National Press Publications
    P.O. Box 419107
    Kansas City, MO 64141-6107

    Fax: 1-913-432-0824
    Phone: 1-800-258-7248
    Internet: www.natsem.com

2. Please print:

    Name_____ Position/Title _____
    Company/Organization_____
    Address_____City _____
    State/Province_____ZIP/Postal Code _____
    Telephone (____)_____ Fax (____) _____
    Your e-mail: _____

3. Easy payment:

    ❑ Enclosed is my check or money order for $_____ (total from back).
    Please make payable to National Press Publications.

    Please charge to:
    ❑ MasterCard   ❑ VISA   ❑ American Express

    Credit Card No. _____ Exp. Date_____
    Signature_____

● ●

MORE WAYS TO SAVE:

SAVE 33%!!! BUY 20-50 COPIES of any title ... pay just $9.95 each ($11.25 Canadian).

SAVE 40%!!! BUY 51 COPIES OR MORE of any title ... pay just $8.95 each ($10.25 Canadian).

* $17.00 in Canada

Buy 3, get 1 FREE!
60-MINUTE TRAINING SERIES™ HANDBOOKS

TITLE	RETAIL PRICE	QTY	TOTAL
8 Steps for Highly Effective Negotiations #424	$14.95		
Assertiveness #4422	$14.95		
Balancing Career and Family #4152	$14.95		
Common Ground #4122	$14.95		
Delegate for Results #4592	$14.95		
The Essentials of Business Writing #4310	$14.95		
Everyday Parenting Solutions #4862	$14.95		
Exceptional Customer Service #4882	$14.95		
Fear & Anger: Slay the Dragons … #4302	$14.95		
Fundamentals of Planning #4301	$14.95		
Getting Things Done #4112	$14.95		
How to Coach an Effective Team #4308	$14.95		
How to De-Junk Your Life #4306	$14.95		
How to Handle Conflict and Confrontation #4952	$14.95		
How to Manage Your Boss #493	$14.95		
How to Supervise People #4102	$14.95		
How to Work With People #4032	$14.95		
Inspire & Motivate: Performance Reviews #4232	$14.95		
Listen Up: Hear What's Really Being Said #4172	$14.95		
Motivation and Goal-Setting #4962	$14.95		
A New Attitude #4432	$14.95		
The New Dynamic Comm. Skills for Women #4309	$14.95		
The Polished Professional #4262	$14.95		
The Power of Innovative Thinking #428	$14.95		
The Power of Self-Managed Teams #4222	$14.95		
Powerful Communication Skills #4132	$14.95		
Present With Confidence #4612	$14.95		
The Secret to Developing Peak Performers #4692	$14.95		
Self-Esteem: The Power to Be Your Best #4642	$14.95		
Shortcuts to Organized Files & Records #4307	$14.95		
The Stress Management Handbook #4842	$14.95		
Supreme Teams: How to Make Teams Work #4303	$14.95		
Thriving on Change #4212	$14.95		
Women and Leadership #4632	$14.95		

Sales Tax

All purchases subject to state and local sales tax.
Questions?
Call
1-800-258-7248

Subtotal	$
Add 7% Sales Tax (Or add appropriate state and local tax)	$
Shipping and Handling ($3 one item; 50¢ each additional item)	$
TOTAL	$